The Holistic Puppy

by Diane Stein

THE CROSSING PRESS
FREEDOM, CALIFORNIA

Puppy Socialization Chart, page 52: Reproduced from THE PERFECT PUPPY: How to Raise a Well-Behaved Dog copyright (c) 1995 The Reader's Digest Association, Inc. Used by permission of the The Reader's Digest Association, Inc.

For information on bulk purchases or group discounts for this and other Crossing Press titles, please contact our Special Sales Manager at 800/777-1048.

Visit our Web site on the Internet: www.crossingpress.com

The alternative healing methods of this book are not meant to take the place of expert veterinary care. When your pet is ill, consult a holistic veterinarian.
The author and publisher accept no responsibility for any loss, damage, injury, or inconvenience sustained by any person or pet as a result of using the training methods outlined herein this book.

Library of Congress Cataloging-in-Publication Data

Diane, Stein, 1948-
    The holistic puppy : how to have a happy, healthy dog / by Diane
Stein for the Crossing Press.
      p. cm.
    Includes bibliographical references (p.   ) and index.
    ISBN 0-89594-946-6 (pbk.)
    1. Puppies. 2. Puppies--Health. 3. Puppies--Diseases-
-Alternative treatment. 4. Dogs. 5. Dogs--Health. 6. Dogs-
-Diseases--Alternative treatment. 7. Veterinary holistic medicine.
I. Title.
SF425.S74   1998
636.7'0893--dc21

98-26917
CIP

For Copper, My Philosopher,
Kali, My Best Girl

and for Sue

acknowledgments

Books are written alone, but they usually cannot be written without the help of others. I would like to thank holistic veterinarians Wendy Thacher-Jensen, DVM, and Karen Bernstein and Larry Bernstein, VMD, for their ideas and protocols on puppy veterinary care, particularly on the controversial subject of vaccinations. Dr. Bernstein provided the very important Dr. Pitcairn articles on vaccinosis. Luc Chaltin and Miki Bell of Newton Homeopathic Laboratories and Allen Kratz, Pharm.D., of HVS Laboratories, also contributed vaccination and vaccinosis antidote information. Central Animal Hospital, St. Petersburg, FL, offered information on standard puppy protocols. Karen Silverman and Prince tried diatomaceous earth for worming and told me that it works. Corinne Nichols reminded me about puppy (and kitty) nicknames.

Kali and Copper supervised the whole writing process. Copper said it was his job to do that and Kali does anything Copper does.

contents

illustrations

kali, copper & co.

Animals are our teachers, the bridges between ourselves and the Earth. Early and pre-industrialized people lived intimately and cooperatively with the Earth and with animals, first with the wild creatures they hunted for survival and later more closely with the farm animals they had to tend. Today most people do not live in cooperation with the Earth and with her creatures; they have traded living nature for inanimate and cold technology. Often our only remaining link to nature and the planet is through the pets we share our homes with, primarily dogs and cats. The pets that most fully interact with humans, that admit humans intimately into their own families and packs, are dogs. Many people's only link with the living Earth, therefore, is our dogs.

Integrating the Pack and the Family

Dogs admit people into their families. Humans believe that it's the other way around, but this is not true from the dog's point of view. From the very start, even the smallest puppy creates its canine social order from the humans who adopt it. She begins immediately to create a dog pack in her new surroundings. Every canine instinct drives the puppy to do this. Her canine pack, taken from her when she leaves her mother and litter mates, is exchanged for a human family, since cooperative pack society is the only reasonable life order for a dog. If the puppy doesn't have this order with others of her kind, she will create it wherever she lives. This is the reason humans choose to live with dogs.

From the human point of view, the new puppy must adapt to human ways, she does not live with a pack of dogs. In living together, humans and animal become a new kind of inter-species order, a canine-human pack-family. The puppy can no longer live entirely by dog-pack rules but must also learn human ones. She must be house-trained, must learn to respect human property and all human be-ings, must accept restraint and walk quietly on a leash, must obey a variety of rules and commands, and must learn to live in harmony with her people and with any other animals that also live in the home. By training a puppy with the understanding that the human family is the dog's pack, the puppy can be taught a social order that she can understand and cooperate with, and she then becomes a joy to live with. With this understanding by both dog and humans, the puppy becomes a full member of the human family and the family becomes the puppy's canine pack, as well. The mutual exchange brings humans back into cooperative contact with animals and the Earth, and gives the puppy the social order/family/pack she is happiest and healthiest living in.

It is this ability to create a human-canine pack together that makes dogs fit so completely into human life. No other animal lives so intimately with people. No other animal has as much to teach us about harmony, loyalty, cooperation, dignity, and hard work, and about creating a stable society as do dogs. By honoring the dog's point of view and raising the new puppy in accordance with it, people and animals learn to relate peacefully and easily. They learn about each other, about creating a family, and about what co-creative life on Earth means. The arrangement helps both dogs and people to evolve physically, emotionally, mentally, and spiritually. Neither species has less to teach or more to learn than the other, unless it be that humans have much more to learn from dogs.

My training and education in pack and family life has come over twenty-five years from five superior Siberian Husky dogs—Cinde, Tiger, Dusty, Copper, and

Kali. Cinde and Tiger were show animals, with Cinde a retired breeder when I got her. Dusty was born in my kitchen from the only litter I myself bred, and Copper and Kali were purebred pound rescues who had both been badly abused. Each dog came to me with his or her own way of approaching life and of creating a family and a pack. Each had a part in training and socializing the dogs that came to me later, as I have usually lived with more than one animal at a time. Each has been a comfort, friend, and family member to me, a more-than-pet whose life I have fully cherished and protected to the best of my ability. They all have taught me patiently, wisely, and well.

My Canine Family Tree

Cinde was a kennel and show dog that came to live with me three days after I moved into my first apartment. I had not been allowed animals while I lived with my parents, so having pets was an immediate priority for me. I met and admired a red-and-white Siberian Husky at a dog show and after much searching ended up with the show dog's mother. I quickly fell in love with the breed's gentleness, friendliness, intelligence, lack of body odor, yodeling talk, bright color, and unusual blue eyes. Cinde was nearly four years old when I took her home. She had championship points and had borne two litters but had difficulty in whelping. I learned later that she was slated to be euthanized the next week and would have died had I not come looking for a beautiful pet at just the right time.

As an adult kennel dog who had never lived indoors, Cinde presented a challenge. She was not house-trained, though she learned willingly and quickly. She did not know how to climb or descend stairs and was afraid of them. I lived in a second-floor apartment. For many days she refused to walk though one particular doorway inside the house and for weeks refused to step past my stereo speakers, whether they were on or off. Missing the confined kennel existence that was all she had known and the dogs she shared an outdoor run and doghouse with, she also refused to eat and proved destructive when left alone.

At the breeder's urging I obtained a show crate, which Cinde felt secure and safe in, and the destructiveness stopped. I didn't even have to close the door: she went into it and stayed there on her own. The breeder also insisted that Cinde would start eating within a few days. She said to put food down once or twice daily, removing it in half an hour whether she had eaten it or not. I did this but for three long weeks Cinde refused to eat anything at all. I was worried and afraid. I had grown to love the beautiful and gentle dog and thought I'd have to take her back to her kennel (to a terrible fate I didn't know about at that time). Finally, after several weeks of her eating nothing or close to it I tearfully resorted to force feeding. Cinde hated that; it disturbed her dignity and her mourning for her old home.

We finally made a deal one evening sitting together on the kitchen floor— that if she would eat enough to be healthy I would get her a puppy. It was my first attempt at human-animal communication; I sat on the linoleum stroking the dog and stating aloud and in my mind the terms of my bargain. Cinde went to her bowl and finished the food. I kept my promise and brought Tiger home, daughter of Cinde's sister Cory, at five and a half weeks of age. Immediately Cinde grew happier: she was a mother again. She began to eat normally and to train and mother her puppy. She made her peace with apartment living. The puppies that she trained while she lived with me were well behaved, cooperative, intelligent, and dignified. Only after she died and I had to raise a dog without her did I realize how much she had been their mother and how much of the training she had done.

I took Cinde, and Tiger as she grew, to puppy conformation matches and a small number of dog shows. Cinde had friends everywhere who recognized her when she greeted them. They didn't know me but everyone knew Cinde. She walked into a show ring as if she owned it, leading me on a leash to follow as she showed herself. She took great pride in herself and in her beauty and she loved the shows. Cinde died at only nine years old of ovarian cancer. My vet operated on her for what looked like a recalcitrant abscess but I knew it was more. The incision never fully healed and tumors developed along the incision line almost immediately. When it seemed she no longer could enjoy her life I made the agonizing decision to have her euthanized. Though she had only been with me for five years, I missed her terribly for a very long time. Among many other things she taught me patience, an appreciation for beauty, and how to raise puppies.

Tiger came for Cinde to mother as a very tiny pup. She was black and white with a soft fluffy coat, turquoise eyes, a freckled muzzle, and striped markings on her chest that gave her the name. She never became a large dog and always kept the size and demeanor of an inquisitive and very mischievous puppy. Tiger was the most intelligent of the dogs who have lived with me and I've often suspected that she was not a dog but a spirit guide embodied as one. Tiger was my teacher from start to finish and as stubborn as she had to be to do it. I loved her passionately. She was noisy as a puppy but from the age of six months stopped using her voice at all. I heard her howl only once as an adult, when she called her puppies to her to nurse during their weaning.

Though quiet and well-behaved, Tiger got into everything. I rescued her from falling in the toilet at eight weeks old. As an adult she liked to turn on the faucets in the bathroom sink and tub and play in the water, usually during the night. When the water got too hot, she would climb into bed, shake water on me, and tell me I could shut it off. Once at a dog show when I wasn't paying enough attention to her trailing behind me, I looked back to find her carrying a three-foot-long rawhide bone. I had to retrace our steps to find who she'd stolen it from and return it. She personally tested every dog food being offered at the sales booths. In the ring, while the judges were measuring her (she barely made the breed's minimum height limit and they measured her at every show), she quietly ate the flowers of their corsages. In show she took a lot of seconds but no one minded. She was fun to go places with.

Tiger worshipped cats. She was terribly disappointed if a cat she approached wouldn't play with her and most of them wouldn't. One of her best friends was a realistic stuffed lion she met in a toy store that we visited occasionally. If we walked in the neighborhood of the store she always led me to it. She loved other dogs and could play, unsupervised, with a friend's rabbit, extremely unusual in a Siberian Husky. She stayed very close to me and was the only Siberian I've had who could be trusted off-lead. At home or away she insisted on touching me at all times, day and night, no matter what I was doing.

Though she didn't use her voice, Tiger was never silent. She talked in my mind continually, a running commentary on everything she did and saw. The dog had definite opinions on any subject. I heard her clearly but was almost unaware of it, her chatter was so much a part of my daily life. Only when she died at twelve and the chatter stopped did I realize what she had given me with her speech.

Tiger also gave me my first lessons in energy work and healing. As I made my earliest attempts she would put herself under my right hand to take the energy. On one occasion I had fallen asleep in a park on a yellow jackets' nest and had been bitten badly. I tried to send the nausea and burning of the insects out through my right hand. Tiger insisted on placing herself there, though I repeatedly moved my hand away from her. All at once the dog got up, seemed to stagger and then to shake off, and walked away. The sickness from the dozens of bites left and never returned.

Of all my dogs, I have bred only one litter and Tiger was their mother. Of the six babies, the first was born breached and with the last Tiger bit the umbilical cord too close so the puppy nearly bled to death. In between, it was I who opened amniotic sacks, tied off and cut cords, and got the babies breathing. At ten days Tiger decided she had enough of motherhood and gave them to me to feed. I fed them with formula and an infant's bottle and Cinde did the rest. All six of the puppies lived and Dusty, a light red that could only be described as blonde, stayed to live with Cinde, Tiger, and me.

Dusty was as different from Tiger as night from day. She was quite large, more active, and far less stubborn. She could not be trusted with cats or small animals, liked to nip human babies on their backsides, and wanted to be a leader among the other dogs. Dusty was a greedy eater who lived to eat. She would eat anything and her favorite food was pizza. I could not trust her off-leash but if she got loose I could usually find her at the nearest pizza shop. She had an ability to manifest human food for herself by making it fall off of plates or stove tops. No one believed me when I warned them about her until they saw it happen. She refused to talk to me because she said I was her mom but would talk to others who came into my home.

She and Tiger were inseparable and Dusty only became close to me after Cinde and Tiger both died. Dusty would watch me getting dressed in the morning and we had a howling routine—I would howl at her and she would howl back. This usually ended with some rough-housing, a walk, and a dog biscuit. Dusty was uninterested in teaching or learning; she just wanted to play. She was bright and active but still well-behaved and very easy to manage. Until I got Copper, that is.

I had been looking for another Siberian Husky for some time when the local shelter called to say that they had a red, purebred male available. I didn't want a male but the shelter man said, "Come and get him, lady, we're going to kill him tomorrow." There was nothing else I could do but bring him home. Copper told me his name before I got him in the car. He was friendly, young, and bouncy but in pitiful shape, with a coat like yellow straw and so thin that every rib and vertebrae stuck up. He was about thirteen months old. My vet weighed him in at thirty-eight pounds and he tested for four kinds of intestinal worms. By that night he was back with the vet on IVs and a diagnosis of parvovirus. When I did distance healing for him he informed me he would live and somehow he did. For the next six months, however, he continued to have bloody diarrhea and vomiting, and despite stuffing him he gained only three pounds.

I was writing *All Women Are Healers* at the time and just beginning to learn homeopathy. When Sidney Spinster agreed to supervise the homeopathy chapter, I asked her what I could do for Copper. He'd been to every vet in the city by that time and they'd all suggested euthanasia. She took a very short case study by phone and told me to order *Phosphorus* 12C in liquid form and "just give him a few drops once." The results were magick. The usually restless dog curled up in the kitchen and slept for hours, and the bleeding, diarrhea, and vomiting stopped immediately. After about ten days he started to have a recurrence and I gave him another dose. Again the symptoms stopped and he took his last dose three weeks later. Copper is twelve years old now and I still have his bottle of remedy—he has never needed it again. He weighs seventy-five pounds. When he shed his straw coat his new coat came in a deep rich copper to live up to his name.

Dusty was past ten years old when Copper arrived. If Copper hadn't stolen her food on first meeting, she probably would have liked him better. As it was, they kept up a running rivalry and constant squabbling as long as Dusty lived. He liked to sneak up to yank her tail and she would furiously chase him around the house. He delighted in teasing her and she in pummeling him. At night they would curl up and sleep together but if either saw me looking at them one would get up and move away. Dusty seemed continually enraged by him and he kept teasing her. Now Copper is old and Dusty's younger reincarnation Kali gives it all back to him. It's fun to watch the situation reversed and Copper getting teased.

Copper is the first dog with whom I have had continuous, deliberate, conscious two-way conversations. At first when I'd ask him to stop his wild behavior, his usual answer was "fat chance!" Later on, grown up, Copper turned out to be quite a philosopher. He's informed me that I'm his wife because "We're leading this pack together, aren't we?" He mourned Dusty terribly when Dusty had lung cancer and asked me to put her down. He still remembers her and when asked tells me, "She's still here." Dusty has returned to me as Kali and both dogs are aware of this.

I had been searching for another dog to keep Copper company for about two years when Kali came. A woman who had attended my workshops phoned me and asked, "Are you home? Your dog's coming in by plane tomorrow night." This was the first I heard of Kali, a six-to-eight-month-old red Siberian Husky puppy with blue eyes. Pat found her in a shelter and adopted her for me. When Kali stepped out of her airline box, all I could think of was "She's Dusty, she looks just like Dusty." Communication with the puppy later confirmed it. "I was supposed to find you," she said. I kept the name for her that Pat picked and Kali has tried to live up to it. Kali is the name of an Indian Goddess who is the destroyer of evil. She is tough and a fighter. Copper still tells everyone that "I got him a dog!"

Most of my Siberians have been gentle and quiet, but Kali is anything but. She remains a defiant teenager even though she is almost seven years old. If I tell her to do something, she will automatically do the opposite. If I call her, she walks the other way. She teases Copper continually and often unfairly, though he is a gentleman and has never fought back. She told me her story. She was pushed out of a moving car and left injured on a highway. After some days alone she found a dog to follow home and the dog's owner took her to the California shelter where Pat adopted her for me.

Kali came to me dragging her hind legs and was incontinent for the first four months I had her. I rolled up the rugs and took her for acupuncture and chiropractic treatments, did Reiki with her, and fed her vitamins and homeopathic remedies. She healed physically within a few months but the emotional damage from her former abuse took much longer to heal. She was the teenager from hell and still goes into a flying rage at standard obedience leash corrections or at the sight of a dog grooming brush.

Kali's goal in life is to have all four feet off the ground as often as possible. She can usually be found lying on her back looking for me to scratch her belly, often on a bed or couch where she is not supposed to be. She wants attention from anyone who comes into the house and can be insatiable in demanding it. If visitors come, she will not let Copper approach them to be petted. Despite her dominance or maybe because of it, Kali is all personality, and her posing and possessiveness can be very funny to watch. Like Dusty, she yodels, howls and talks, and is very greedy. She has been an ongoing lesson in patience, problem solving, and physical and emotional healing. We have learned a lot together. Just lately, she's decided that she loves me.

Kali, Copper, Dusty, Tiger, and Cinde will appear throughout this book, describing the lessons they have taught me about dogs and raising puppies. As they are my teachers, it is only appropriate that they be there and be heard. Your new puppy will teach you just as much in his or her own way, but hopefully what I have learned from my Siberian Huskies will help make puppy raising easier for you and for your pet. I have lived in an inter-species family-pack for twenty-five years and learned to listen to the experts on dog raising, the dogs themselves. You will find great delight in doing the same with your puppy.

Before we begin the technical stuff about care, feeding, and training, it is important to learn how to talk with and understand animals. The next chapter teaches you how to talk with your dog, and, more important, how to listen.

talking dog—interspecies communication

One evening I was sitting on the couch eating almonds and Copper was begging for them. "Why should I give a dog almonds?" I asked him. "They're expensive." Copper informed me that dogs are "Great Intergalactic Be-ings," or at least that he is, and that almonds are what such great Be-ings eat. "Nice try, Pal," I said, but gave him some. He has continued to tell me that he is a great intergalactic Be-ing but says that Kali "is just a dog." Those are fighting words for Kali, who insists that she is a "girl" and that calling her a dog is an insult. "He's calling me that bad word again," she tattles. "Make him stop." This usually precedes a scuffle, with Kali furious and Copper pleased that he's succeeded in making her angry.

A Far-Reaching Range of Communication

I hear both dogs clearly in my mind as I hear my own thoughts. They speak to me in their own voices, using words and ideas not my own. I usually have to focus and concentrate to hear them. The dogs talk to me only when they are at rest but not asleep and they talk to me only when they choose to. If I ask Copper something he doesn't want to tell me, he says, "Go away. I'm sleepy now." Dogs consider people uneducated and therefore in need of their protection, mainly because most people don't talk to them. They think we can't or won't. One dog I met on a workshop trip was delighted and surprised to talk with me. "I didn't know people could talk," she said. Most animals, wild or tame, will talk with humans who make the effort and most are surprised when we try it.

Dogs talk to each other telepathically in the same way and can do so long distance. Copper talks to Kali, usually to tease her, and to other dogs as well. I tried to find out what his range of communication is. "Can you talk to a dog who lives three blocks away?" I asked him. "Only if we're friends," said Copper. "Otherwise it's bad manners." I asked, "If a dog is your friend, how far away can he be if you want to talk to him?" "Anywhere," was Copper's reply. "Will you know where the dog is?" I asked. "Maybe." "If a friend is in trouble would you know?" "Sure," said Copper, "but it's bad manners to talk to dogs that aren't your friends." I asked whether he could talk to dogs who were no longer alive and he said he could and did, and that he knew whether they were alive or dead.

A PBS program described dolphins and dogs as having the same evolutionary root ancestor. This seemed far-fetched, so I asked Copper, "What do dogs know about dolphins?" "They're the other kind," said the dog. "Other kind of what?" I asked. "Of Great Intergalactic Be-ing." "Do dogs and dolphins come from the same place?" I asked. Copper said, "Sure." "Where is that, do you know the name?" "No," he said. "Not here." I asked him, "Do dogs talk to dolphins?" "Go away," said Copper, "I'm sleepy." The conversation was over.

The next day, I continued. "What do dogs know about manatees?" Copper said, "Dogs don't know manatees." "Are they Great Intergalactic Be-ings?" I asked. "No," he said. "What about whales?" I continued. "Are they Great Intergalactic Be-ings?" "The other place," said Copper, "[they come from] a different place than dogs and dolphins." I asked him, "Do dogs talk to whales?" He said, "No, dogs know whales, but we don't talk to them." I asked once more about dolphins and again he wouldn't answer.

Later I tried again: "If dogs, whales, and dolphins are Great Intergalactic Be-ings, what about people?" Copper said, "Some of them." "Which ones?" I asked him. "The ones with wings that walk around the living room and don't exist," he replied—angels, in other words—"and the Gold Lady." Gold Lady is Copper's name for Brede, a guide and Goddess. For Copper, discarnate Be-ings like angels and spirit guides are very real but "don't exist," though he can describe them down to the last feather. Copper also has informed me that the little lizards that are everywhere outdoors in Florida don't exist either, but that's really because he can't catch them, and if they don't exist anyway, he loses no pride.

"How about me?" I asked him. "Am I a Great Intergalactic Be-ing?" Said Copper, "I'm not sure." "And what about Kali?" I asked. Copper insists that "she's a dog" just to make Kali angry. It's a prime insult. "Talked to any dolphins lately?" I pressed. "Those things," complained Copper, "they never shut up, they talk all the time!" Dogs apparently do talk to dolphins, or at least the dolphins talk to them.

Obviously dogs have a much wider understanding of existence than humans can even imagine. They communicate with other dogs, and with other species they have no direct experience with. Copper has never met a dolphin or a whale face to face. They talk to Be-ings in and out of earthplane embodiment, both friends who are no longer living and discarnate Be-ings like angels who were never on Earth at all. Dogs' range of communication has no limit of distance or even dimension. They have a clear code about when it is proper to communicate with another Be-ing on or off the Earth. Only the strongest human psychics have the abilities that dogs use in such a casual way. No wonder dogs consider people uneducated.

A Dog's Responsibility to Serve and Protect

They also take their jobs with people very seriously. Annie, a West Highland white terrier, told me that she's the mother of her family of four humans and has total responsibility for their care. She says she runs the household, which includes children, adults, other animals, and a large home and yard. "I have a big responsibility here," she says. "It's very hard work." Her human guardian suspects that Annie is a soul fragment of her mother, sent by her mother to help her run a family. After Annie received Reiki attunements for the first time, she began walking on people who were lying on the floor waiting for healing. She watched her human's hands do healing and then used her paws the same way.

Once you begin communicating with your dog, you will find it very hard to disrespect her as a "dumb animal." As the communication bond develops, it becomes very clear that dogs have intelligence at least equal to, if different from, that of people. They have a perspective that is simple but highly evolved and very clear. Dogs have souls, karma, spirit guides, and a developed chakra system and aura. Their soul structure is the same as that of humans and their oversouls are human/angels. They may be fragments of our own core souls or of souls separate from us.

This is not to say that they don't have negative emotions, misguided behavior, or maddening personality traits. Like people, they do, and abuse, weak genetics, or bad training can make them worse. They may totally misunderstand what they hear and see in the human situations around them. But also like people, there is much more to our pets (and to all animals) than meets the eye, much more than we "uneducated" humans are usually aware of. A dog's life purpose is strong and clear and the overwhelming passion of her life. This purpose is to serve, love, protect, and educate her human pack and family. Dogs' role in educating human lives is often overlooked but is a dog's primary reason for living and Be-ing. Cooperative living and awareness of the oneness of all life is a given for any dog who has been allowed to express her life purpose. This is the main message she has for her human pack, and she is totally responsible to that purpose.

Dogs also protect people in more ways than are normally understood. While barking at strangers who come into her pack-family territory and frightening off burglars is part of her job, so is energy protection. Dogs take on and transmute the negative emotions of the people around them and provide a buffer in disharmonious households. If you are sick or upset, your dog will know it and try to help. She may do so by clowning for you, by placing her body in between you and what she perceives as danger to you, or by taking the pain into herself. She also takes into her own body and emotions unseen energies that may be negative to people or disruptive to her home. While a vigorous adult dog can usually transmute this negativity unharmed, thereby protecting her people from it and releasing it, puppies and older or ill dogs may not be able to do this. They can become sick and even die while protecting their humans from harm.

Our dogs also have thorough knowledge and understanding of human personalities. Not only can we communicate with them, but they hear our thoughts and understand them according to their own experience. I can lie in bed without moving in the morning, but as soon as my mind starts working Kali and Copper come looking for me to let them outside. If I'm sitting quietly and think about taking them for a walk, both dogs come from anywhere in the house to sit at the front door expectantly. Dare to think about moving to a new house and watch your animals get visibly upset. Some of this is body language and some telepathy. We can hide nothing from them.

I once joined in a conversation about moving with a woman whose miniature dachshund was in the room. Tara was eleven years old and had been with her person since puppyhood. The woman talked about placing the dog in another home when she moved out of state. "You can't do that," I said. "She's been with you too long." As she continued, the dog became more and more agitated. "Look at Tara," I said. "She understands everything you're saying." The woman refused to recognize the little dog's awareness. "Tara," I said, "if she does this you can come and live with me." Tara then climbed into my lap. The woman moved and took the dog with her, but never acknowledged Tara's clear response to her callousness.

Kali expresses her knowledge of people by giving them names. When she was younger, the names were usually those of other dogs she had known, but as she gets older they become more revealing. She will only name someone who has visited at least a few times, who shows interest in her and plays with her, and only if they ask for it. She names all men "Nice Man," except one who Kali calls "The Boy with Girl's Hair." Her name for a woman who has two cats is "Cat Lady" (her nose tells her all about the cats). To a visitor who has several cats, she said, "Ugh, you stink of cats, you smell!" The woman heard her clearly, and Kali named her "Too Many Cats."

 holistic puppy

One woman, who seems gruff but apparently is not so bad, Kali named "All Bark and No Bite" with an alternate name of "Big Lady," as she is tall. Another friend, unlucky in love, was given the original name of "Fox Lady." When she asked for a different name, Kali dubbed her "The One With the Two Loser Lovers". The woman asked her "Which two?" and opted to keep "Fox Lady" awhile longer. A psychic friend is "Star Lady" and two women are called "Princess." She has named others "Brownie," "Cuddles," "Taste Good," and "Sweet Lady." Copper is "Oh, Him!" and I of course am "Mom."

Kali doesn't like it when I fill the bird feeder or feed the squirrels; she says I shouldn't feed anyone but her. She tries to take Copper's food, too, and refuses to be nice to him until he stops calling her a dog. She eats the spilled birdseed to keep the birds from getting it and it makes her thirsty and gives her a stomach ache. When I asked her what we could do so she wouldn't get sick from eating it, she replied, "You could fill the bird feeder with pretzels."

When I asked her if it would be okay to add another dog to our pack, Kali's answer was, "Only if I'm the best one." We argue about dominance. She insists that she's "the best" and that gives her the right. When a visitor in the house told her to lie down, Kali replied, "No, you lie down. I don't have to do that." She didn't lie down. When I call her I get the same response. The less dominant Copper says that he and I are "running this pack together, aren't we?" Later he told me, "I guess I'll let you do it." Along with higher wisdom, dogs have egos!

How to Read Your Dog's Body Language

Dogs also speak in eloquent and articulate body language, and are fully aware of ours. This physical communication does not need psychic contact. Tara's agitation required neither an animal behaviorist nor a psychic to interpret. A dog's excitement when her person comes home is obvious, as are many other communications. Your puppy or dog watches you. When you are angry, your physical stance says so. Perhaps your hands go to your hips and your facial expression worries her before you speak. When you are happy, you bend down to the animal with arms open and a smile, and your dog reacts accordingly. A smile, by the way, represents a welcome only to humans but dogs learn to comprehend it. When a dog shows her teeth it's usually a threat. Her softer teeth-showing grin with open mouth can mean a joke but is often an expression of submission.

A relaxed dog with ears and head up, mouth closed, and tail held down is calm and ready for whatever may come. Her tail held high means confidence and pride. If her ears go back and tail raises slightly, the dog is less certain; she may be worried, tentative, or questioning. A tail held down and tucked under her hind legs expresses submission. When the dog's facial expression tenses, her forehead wrinkles, and her ears draw back tightly against her head, the dog is suspicious and feeling threatened. If in addition, her lips pull back and tail fluffs out, she is on the defensive; add the sight of fangs, raised hackles, and a lowered head, and she is likely to charge or bite.

There are gentle expressions and body positions, too. People can imitate these and your dog or puppy will understand you. If your puppy's front legs are on the floor and her rump is in the air, she's inviting you to play; her tail will likely be wagging and she may bark or yodel. She may pant though she is not over-heated, or paw at you; these are also invitations to play. Mimic her position, pant, or paw back and the game begins. A gaily held, wagging tail is an expression of friendliness, curiosity, or another invitation for you to play with her.

If her tail is held low and wagging, she is expressing submission to you. Further submission, commonly seen in puppies, shows the dog crouched down or rolled over on her back with throat and belly exposed. She may urinate or dribble but do not punish her as this is a communication, not a house-training problem. Ignore it. As she grows older and more confident the dribbling will stop. Submissive postures are instinctual in puppies; they are not caused by fear and should not *be* caused by making the puppy afraid of you in any way. In the puppy's litter, these postures engage the mother dog's protection and caretaking; in the human family, the puppy uses the same communications to engage yours.

Likewise, a young puppy will crowd against you when you come home to her. When she did that with her canine mother, the mother dog provided food. A small puppy may also be mounted by older dogs in the family, not as a sexual act

The Dog's Major Facial Expressions[1]

Calm

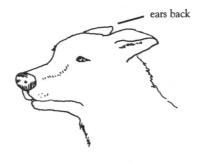

ears back

Worried

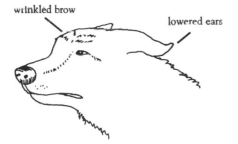

wrinkled brow

lowered ears

Suspicious

threat stare

lips pulled back

Defensive

fangs exposed

Ready to Bite

Remorseful

1 Jean Craighead George, *How to Talk to Your Dog*, (New York, NY, Warner Books, 1985), p. 68,
and Diane Stein, *Natural Healing for Dogs and Cats*, (Freedom, CA, The Crossing Press, 1993),
p. 35.

The Dog's Tail Positions[2]

Questioning

Confident

Submissive

Ready to Fight

Tentative

Calm

2 Jean Craighead George, *How to Talk to Your Dog*, (New York, NY, Warner Books, 1985), p. 81, and Diane Stein, *Natural Healing for Dogs and Cats*, (Freedom, CA, The Crossing Press, 1993), p. 36.

but to engage the puppy's submission. Let the two of them work it out as long as neither is being hurt. As the puppy matures she will find her social position with the family's other pets.

None of these submissive postures are to be imitated by people. In the human pack, the dog takes a child's role permanently. The dog is subordinate to the people in the family and this is necessary and also natural. A dog who refuses the submissive role and tries to be an alpha pack leader in the human family can become a serious behavior problem as she matures.[3]

You will quickly become aware of your puppy's facial expressions, body language, vocal speech, and their messages. A dog's eyes speak volumes of what she is feeling and thinking, as well. Your observation and understanding of these is part of bonding with your pet and will increase her bonding with you.

Opening to Inter-Species Communication

It is also easy to learn psychic communication, inter-species communication, with your dog or puppy and I highly recommend learning this skill. Doing so opens a new world for most "uneducated" humans and begins your education in respect for the oneness of all life. Your relationship with your puppy or dog will become even more valuable when you can speak to each other fully. You are your dog's mother, Goddess, and purpose in life; honor her commitment to you by opening your ears to her needs.

To do this requires quiet practice for a short time each day. The last thing before bedtime is good, as is any time you can sit quietly near your pup while she is resting but not asleep. Do not expect your dog to respond when she is busy doing things important to being a dog, such as eating, playing, or on alert to someone at the door. Do not expect to hear her when you are likewise engaged. Both human and puppy must be quiet, relaxed, and not busy with other things.

It is important that you approach your pet with great respect on every occasion. If you sneer at her, scold her, or threaten her in any way, you will be ignored, and it will be harder to gain her response later. Like a human baby, a puppy's level of understanding and response will be that of a baby or a child. This is perfectly

3 Carol Lea Benjamin, *Mother Knows Best, The Natural Way to Train Your Dog*, (New York, NY, Howell Book House, 1985), p. 53-54.

normal. She and her communication with you will mature by the time she is two years old.

Begin by sitting quietly near your resting dog. Focus your mind upon her in a relaxed but concentrated way that excludes other perceptions and distractions. Look at her but do not expect your puppy to look at you, though she may. Animal communication is a light meditative state and the skill is equivalent to speaking with your spirit guides or higher self. If you are familiar with this form of meditation, use it on your pet and you will reach her easily.

Clear all other thoughts from your mind and hold only one thought, your dog's name. Repeat it in your mind gently and at low volume several times. She will hear you. You may be aware of a response in body language, pictures appearing in your mind, or in words. Then, with your mind held clear of other thoughts, think slowly and clearly "I love you" and the dog's name. Wait for the response, still keeping your mind clear. Tell her you are glad she is living with you, that you appreciate her, that you will do your best to take good care of her and make her happy. Wait for a while and listen. Whether you perceive a response or not, go over to the puppy, quietly stroke her, and end the session.

Try this every night until you are comfortable with it and you feel that your puppy is at least listening. If she is not responding, ask her if she'd be willing to talk with you or to teach you to hear her. Most dogs can't resist a chance to teach a person and if she feels you are sincere she is likely to respond. The dog may communicate with you in pictures rather than words or in colors or feelings that she sends to you. A small puppy may begin with, or be capable of, only giggles. Accept your perceptions and don't disbelieve what you feel or hear. Take it slowly and in short sessions, relax with it, and do not insist or force the pet's response. The skill will come in time, as any form of meditation takes some practice. As your communication develops and evolves, your conversations will become fuller and more satisfying.

The skill of inter-species communication is important for any pet guardian who wishes to fully understand her dog or puppy. It is a skill worth learning and using, and it offers great rewards for dog and human both.

choosing your puppy or dog

Many people choose a pet on impulse. They see an adorable puppy and can't resist bringing it home. Yet choosing a companion for the next dozen years or more should not be done lightly or impulsively. A puppy is a great responsibility. Careful thought before adoption leads to greater happiness later with a dog that truly fits your home and family's needs. There are many different kinds of dogs, with a wide variety of personalities, sizes and weights, grooming needs, and temperaments. Most people want a new puppy but the older dog in need of a home may be in dire straits and could potentially be a better pet. Once these decisions are made, which individual puppy or dog is the best for your situation?

Finding the Right Fit

Probably you should decide first what size dog to bring home. Dogs come in all sizes from teacup toy Chihuahuas to two-hundred-pound mastiffs and Saint Bernards. If you live in an apartment or are elderly or handicapped, a smaller breed is far more practical than a giant one that needs more exercise and space. Some apartment complexes that allow pets have size limits for dog residents. If you have a large yard and an active lifestyle, however, a large dog may be right for you. If you have small children, a tiny toy dog may be too fragile for living with them. Small breeds other than the tiniest have longer life-spans than very large breeds. A miniature pinscher I knew as a child lived to be twenty-one years old. Some large breeds are old dogs at only six or eight years of age. Most medium breeds have a life expectancy today of ten to fourteen years old.

If your resources are limited, be aware of the cost difference in maintaining small and large dogs after the initial purchase price, which is relatively the same. The larger dog eats more and will cost more for veterinary care, grooming, and kennel boarding where price is determined by the animal's weight. Supplies like food supplements, crates, collars, toys and bowls also cost more, and while the differences may seem unimportant they add up. A larger dog requires more training, since bad behavior or destructiveness in a big dog cannot be tolerated as it often is in a small one. A toy or small breed dog can simply be picked up if it misbehaves. Total obedience is less crucial. Formal obedience training is more necessary for a bigger dog and the classes are also an expense.

Small dogs are not for everyone. As a former dog groomer, I was always aware that my most difficult customers were small dogs. The big ones were more placid, more biddable, better trained and better behaved, and generally had better temperaments. Their weight made them harder to get in and out of the washing tub but they were generally much easier to handle. A three-pound toy poodle sent me bleeding to the emergency room by pulling my thumbnail off. The only dog I ever recognized as truly vicious was a terrier who weighed under twenty pounds. Some small dogs are highly strung and they can be nervous and yappy. Some may be temperamentally unsafe around children, where many larger and sturdier animals make better baby-sitters and nannies. The issue here is preference.

If you want a dog for a particular purpose, it may determine the size and breed. Someone interested in tracking requires a dog whose instincts and talent differ from those of dogs needed for sled-pulling. A person who wants a dog for protection must choose an animal bred for that job, and be careful to choose an individual who is not overly nervous, dominant, or aggressive. A well-bred

German shepherd, Doberman pinscher, or Rottweiler may do here, where a greyhound could not perform adequately. Likewise the dog that is wanted for any other work from nanny to sheep-herding must come from a breed with those inbred instincts and heritage. A chow chow may be too active and aggressive to raise with toddlers and a Great Dane too placid for police work. A Shetland sheepdog may be too vocal for apartment complex living, but makes a wonderful dog for obedience, and a digging dachshund would not be welcomed by an avid gardener but would also keep moles and gophers away.

Energy and Temperament Levels

Some active protection breeds, herding dogs, and terriers are a perfect match for owners who jog. Dalmatians also fall into this category. A couch potato dog like a borzoi does well with less action and a little bit of movement goes a long way for a tiny Maltese's short legs. A very placid dog, especially once she's older, may not want to run and a tiny one may become exhausted quickly. These are things to consider for the prospective dog guardian. How much exercise does the person like, and can she take her dog with her? An energetic dog with too little exercise becomes unhappy, destructive, and may develop behavior problems. For this dog, a fenced yard is necessary but probably not enough. Don't adopt a dog from a very active breed unless you can give her what she needs.

Some breeds are also more obedient than others. Dogs used for seeing-eye work are a good guideline; golden retrievers, Labrador retrievers, German shepherds, and Doberman pinschers, as well as all the hunting breeds, are easily trained. If you have ever watched a show ring obedience competition, you will see these breeds, as well as numerous Shetland sheepdogs and poodles (all sizes). Siberian Huskies, other northern breeds, or basenjis are not willingly obedient. However lovable and loving, they are stubborn, difficult to confine, have short attention spans, and are much more independent. Their person's approval may be secondary to something else they'd rather do. They are not easily trained and harsh training can ruin their temperaments. Those that do well in obedience work can still rarely be let off-leash at home. A person who insists her dog be reliably obedient would be unhappy with a breed that cannot offer that. It depends on what is important to you.

Many books are available that describe the characteristics and personalities of the different breeds. They give the dogs' size and weight range, what work the breed was developed to do, how much exercise they need, and how easy or difficult they are to train. While no book can tell you exactly what an individual dog will be like, they are a good beginning. Once you have decided what breed fits your size and lifestyle needs, talk to a breeder of the dogs you are interested in. She can offer information not found in books and further confirm or narrow your breed choice. She may also have a puppy or adult dog that meets your needs.

Show Dogs and Working Dogs

If you choose a purebred dog, you may also need to decide whether you want a show quality animal, pet quality, or a dog from a field work or obedience bloodline. There can be major differences here, in price, conformation, appearance, function, and even size. Show quality means that the dog is competitive with others of its type in closeness to the breed ideal or standard. Such dogs are prospective show animals and breeding stock and will not be spayed or neutered. Expect to pay at least $500 for a show potential puppy and more for a ring-proven grown dog. Whether an unproven puppy or dog has show potential or not is usually estimated by the breeder but in a young puppy the judgment is always a gamble. A reputable breeder, best found at a dog show or from advertising in breed or show journals, is the only advisable purchase source if you wish for a show quality dog.

The puppies and dogs that a kennel determines are inadequate for show or breeding are called pet quality. They are wonderful animals and often exceptionally beautiful but are less likely to make successful show dogs. A dog may be determined pet quality because she is smaller or larger than the ideal for her breed, may have an unacceptable color or color pattern, or may have other physical characteristics that the layperson would find irrelevant. She may be a dog that did not do well in shows, or like my Cinde, may be a breeding animal with difficulty whelping or whose puppies were not show potential. These lovely dogs cost less than show prospects but can still cost a few hundred dollars. A dog that is not show potential for conformation may do wonderfully in obedience competition. Most breeders require that a pet quality animal be spayed or neutered, as only the best physical specimens are used for breeding.

A dog from a field dog line has been bred for work, rather than show. Usually this means hunting, tracking, herding, or sled-pulling. It can also mean obedience. The dogs may be larger than what is acceptable in a show animal of their breed or smaller (as in seeing-eye golden retrievers). Conformation—physical beauty—is secondary to the animal's potential for being excellent at doing her breed's job. These dogs usually have highly developed instincts for their profession and would be unhappy if not permitted to participate in it. A field dog bred for retrieving, for example, will be frustrated and unhappy if she is never taken hunting and given outlet for her inbred instincts. A field bred hunter needs to be hunted, a tracker needs to track, and a herding dog needs to herd (or she will herd your children in the living room!). If interested in one of these, ask yourself if you can keep her occupied and happy doing her work.

Lifestyle Considerations

In choosing a breed, be aware of the care that a particular type of dog needs and what is acceptable for the person who will be the dog's caretaker. Some breeds shed more than others, for example. Siberian Huskies and other northern breeds (keeshond, Samoyed, malamute, Norwegian elkhound, spitz) have thick double coats that come out in tufts and handfuls twice or so a year. There is so much hair that it can actually be spun into wool for sweaters. Are you a strict housekeeper or one that can live with fur everywhere for months at a time, however soft and clean that fur might be?

Many double-coated and long-haired breeds require a great deal of grooming. Old English sheepdogs are the groomers' classic specimen. Some long-coated canines require daily combing and brushing to prevent the hair from becoming a mess of mats and tangles; Afghan hounds, Lhasa Apsos, and Maltese come to mind. Are you willing to do it? Some people have these dogs clipped, rather than do the work, but why adopt a dog for its lovely coat and then cut the coat off?

Poodles, on the other hand, don't shed at all. They require clipping every six weeks. Without it their coats become long, unkempt, and felted. Clipping a dog is not difficult to learn but most pet guardians send their dogs to a grooming shop. This must be done regularly and the cost (about $20 each time) adds up. Terriers and spaniels must also be clipped regularly to keep the look you bought the dog for and to keep the dog neat and healthy. Unclipped poodles and terriers look like woolly lambs, which is fine if you like it, but the dogs must then be kept thoroughly brushed. Ungroomed peekapoos and cockapoos (not purebred dogs) become hopelessly matted, with clumps of felted hair that pull uncomfortably on their skins. Before you choose a breed, inquire what care its coat needs.

Some breeds of dogs are also droolers. Bloodhounds, bassets, beagles, mastiffs, and Saint Bernards come under this category. Look for the dog with the long pendulous lips. Is this a trait that bothers you? Do you mind that the pet's front is usually damp and may leave a damp spot where she's been sleeping? Some dogs have more doggy odor than others and some have none at all. Poodles and northern breeds have little oil in their coats; they may absorb odors from around them but have no body odor of their own. Some hunting dogs, however, usually breeds that retrieve from the water, have very oily coats and strong doggy odors. Does the scent of a dog's coat seem natural to you or do you prefer an odorless breed?

Some dogs have the tendency to be barkers (terriers and herding dogs like shelties) or howlers (beagles, fox hounds and bassets). Do you live close to your neighbors? Can you keep your dog indoors and train it to be quiet? Will barking be a problem if you live in an apartment? Some dogs are more highly strung than others. Cocker spaniels and Irish setters have a strong startle reaction and can become hysterical, and many poorly bred cockers are biters. Overly bred Doberman pinschers can also be nervous biters, not a good trait around children. If you choose these breeds, observe the litter and its mother carefully before selecting a puppy from it. Not all dogs in a breed express a negative trait and those from a reputable breeder may not express it at all. These are things to consider when choosing which dog is right for you.

In searching for your optimal pet don't overlook mixed breeds. They are more of a mystery, as you will not have a characteristics profile to tell you what to expect. You may be surprised at the size the puppy ends up to be or what it will finally look like grown up. All dogs are loyal and loving, however, and the mixed breed on death row at an animal shelter may need you terribly. A mixed-breed dog can be freer of genetic defects than a purebred one but may also have had a more difficult start and harder life than the purebred dog. You will give the same care to either one and love a mixed-breed dog just as much. A pound puppy is cheaper to begin with but after the initial purchase expect it to cost the same amount financially and require as much raising and training.

Once you decide on a breed there are still more choices to make. Do you want a male or a female? Adult dog or puppy? Most people seem to want male dogs, thinking they make better pets, but toy breed males (with the exception of bichon frises) can be snappy around children. In my experience, males tend to be more protective and females more aggressive. Males are larger, stronger, and more impressive looking than the females of a breed. Females are easier to keep at home and can be more involved in their family's daily life. They are usually less headstrong and easier to train. Unless you have a purebred dog of show and breeding quality, expect to neuter or spay your dog before his/her sex-specific characteristics appear. Female heat cycles or male spraying and dominance are to be avoided in a pet, and so is breeding since so many dogs die weekly for lack of homes. The surgery costs approximately the same for males and females.

When thinking of a new dog, most people think of getting a puppy. There are many reasons, however, to adopt a fully grown pet. While a puppy that grows up in your home is trained from the beginning in your ways, a grown dog may require less training, and maybe none at all. She may already be house-trained, or the house-training is done quickly. She probably comes to you with house manners and some obedience training, and an adult dog is usually past the chewing stage (but may still be destructive, especially at first). For someone who works all day or hasn't patience with puppy training and antics, a young adult dog can be ideal.

Whether obtained from an animal shelter, kennel, or a rescue group, adult dogs often have hard luck stories and are very much in need of new homes. They may come to you because a former owner died or could not keep them. They may be victims of neglect and loss. Some are kennel or racetrack rejects whose alternative is death. These are loving, beautiful animals who need homes badly and whose chances for finding them are far slimmer than a pup's. Kennels may euthanize older dogs that are not show or breeding potential. Greyhound racetracks euthanize thousands of dogs a year simply because they are not winners or are past their racing prime though still young. Dogs rescued in this way are fully aware of what you are giving them. They may require some socializing and training, and some healing, but you will find them loving, loyal, and grateful. (Addresses of purebreed rescue referral organizations are located in the Resource section of this book.)

How to Find Your New Best Friend

Now that you've chosen what breed of puppy or dog, where will you go to find it? An animal shelter or friend's litter is the obvious source for a mixed-breed puppy, but what about a purebred one? Pet shop puppies are cute and appealing but not your best choice. Such puppies are taken from their mothers too early, subjected to the traumas of shipping and selling, and may not be socialized or healthy. If you want a purebred puppy it is always best to seek one from a reputable breeder. A breeder will be able to show you the puppy's mother to give you an idea of her offspring's type and temperament. If you have chosen a large breed dog, look for litters whose parents have been OFA (Orthopedic Foundation for Animals) certified, which means they have had their hips checked for inheritable dysplasia. If you have chosen a breed that may develop eye problems look for puppies whose parents are registered normal with CERF (Canine Eye Registration Foundation).

The breeder will also provide you with a blue AKC puppy registration form, which, when sent in with the puppy's name, will register your dog as a purebred with the American Kennel Club. If you adopt an adult, the breeder will provide you with a white signed transfer of ownership for the AKC. She will also provide you with health records of vaccinations and worming and other information about your individual dog or puppy and its breed that you will find valuable. If your dog is a pet quality adult, the breeder may require the dog to be spayed or neutered before she releases her or his papers.

Finally you have done all your homework and get to meet your dog or puppy. It's taken a lot of decisions and searching to come this far. How do you know which puppy in a litter of cute babies will make the best pet for your family-pack? Most people are told to take the first puppy that walks up to them but this can be problematic. The first puppy that comes up to you is usually the boldest in the litter and may also be the most aggressive. She may decide as she grows up to run the pack and try to take over your family, a perfect situation for training and behavior difficulties. Most people are also told to avoid the runt in the corner that's too shy to be friendly. Your goal and best bet is the puppy in between.

Look for the puppy, or adult dog of any breed, that neither rushes you first nor hangs back until last. When you call her, she hesitates and watches for a moment before she comes to you. Her tail may be held low or high, but her head is up and she doesn't cringe or shrink away. She is alert and watching you, cautious but unafraid. When you hold your hand out to this puppy, she will not lick or bite at it, but sniffs and then looks up to you for your cues of what to do next. If you throw a squeaky toy or wad of paper on the floor she will not be the first in the litter to approach it, nor will she be the last. She will test out the new object before she pounces on it. When you think you have spotted this puppy, take her into a quiet room away from the others and see how she reacts to you. The puppy to look for is one that is friendly but not pushy, who checks you out before she relates to you fully.

Alone with your puppy, make the following tests: 1) Kneel down and call her, clapping your hands. Your ideal puppy will come readily and quietly, tail held low or high. She will not jump up or mouth you; 2) Stand up and walk away. Your ideal puppy will follow readily but not get underfoot; 3) Roll the pup over on her back and hold her gently on the floor or ground for thirty seconds. This is called the alpha roll-over. Your ideal puppy's reaction will be to struggle for a moment and then lie quietly until you let her get up. She may or may not look up at you; 4) Look for the same reaction when you lift the puppy just off the ground, holding her up safely but away from you for another thirty seconds; 5) Allow the puppy to stand on the ground again and stroke her repeatedly from head to back. Your ideal puppy's reaction is not to jump, paw, or bite, but to cuddle up to you and lick your face or hands.[1]

The puppy you have chosen by these standards is about a number three or four on a dominance scale of six. A number one or two puppy will rush up to you first, jump on you, get underfoot, and bite, lick, or paw at your hands. When rolled over or held up in restraint, she struggles and thrashes and will not settle down. This puppy grown up will be more dominant and aggressive than most families find comfortable. The dog will run the household, resist training, be headstrong and possibly destructive. My Kali is a number two.

At the other end of the scale, a number five or six puppy is the shy one who hesitates, waits until all the others have arrived, or doesn't come to you at all. She hides or is uninterested. When you walk away for her to follow, she either stays away or comes hesitantly and reluctantly with her tail down. When rolled over or elevated she doesn't struggle or resist and may strongly avoid your eye contact. Held up, she may freeze or lick your hands. When stroked, the puppy rolls over or goes away from you and stays away. This puppy is not aggressive enough; she has little inborn self-confidence. She will not be able to hold her own in the human or animal family-pack. She will be shy of people and new experiences, and, treated badly or insensitively, could become a fear biter. Be aware, however, that members of some dog breeds that are less people oriented will remain aloof from strangers. They will not hide or cringe but may ignore you. You can observe this behavior in northern breed puppies, and it is natural for them. Once the dog knows you, it's a different story.

For most breeds, the puppy to adopt is the median between extremes, the one in the middle. Copper is a three. This is the puppy that checks out a situation

1 Adapted from the Puppy Aptitude Test in: The Monks of New Skete, *The Art of Raising a Puppy*, (Boston, New York, Toronto, and London, Little Brown and Company, 1991), p. 262.

holistic puppy

before reacting to it, then comes to you unafraid. She hesitates but does not cringe, and she accepts your authority (gives up the struggle when restrained) as leader of her pack. This puppy will use intelligence in her reactions to daily life, and will accept training in good grace. She looks before she leaps and lets you make the decisions. Trained and treated gently, she will be the ideal pet. She will not make it as a police or guard dog (choose a one or two for that), but will protect her family adequately and be safe and loyal in your home. What more could anyone want in a companion and housemate for the next ten to fifteen years? This number three or four puppy is the one to take home and love.

While these tests are suitable only for young puppies, in choosing an adult dog watch for the basic traits. Look for a dog that is cautious but unafraid, that reacts without aggressiveness or cringing, that watches you and accepts your cues and lead. Do not try the roll-over or elevation exercises with an unknown adult dog. Instead, observe her reactions to you and be aware of her body language to assess her.

Now that you have finally found your dog or puppy, let's take her home and move her into your life.

coming home

The first day and night with a new pup or grown dog are exciting and stressful for all concerned. It helps to have the things you need beforehand to prevent additional rushing around. Though everyone wants to pet and play with the new family member, it helps to make the homecoming as quiet as possible for the new dog. New sights, smells, places, people, and the travel itself are overwhelming to her. Keep things simple the first day. If she has never seen a leash, carry her for now. This is not the day for a bath or grooming, even if she is very dirty, Training, including the all-crucial house-training, can wait one day longer. Never scold a puppy or dog on her first day with you—tomorrow is soon enough. Never, ever hit a puppy or dog.

Preparing for Your New Arrival

You will need some basic supplies whether your dog is a puppy or adult. These can be found easily at pet shops or ordered from mail-order suppliers. A few of the things may come from the supermarket but for the most part grocery store pet supplies are low quality for the price. You will never buy dog food there. Some items can wait until later but most are best to have on hand from the start. The beginning cash outlay seems like a lot, but the majority of the purchases will last a long time if chosen properly—many of them for the life of your dog.

The most important, most expensive thing to buy is a dog cage, called a crate. If your pet was air-shipped from a kennel, she will come in a closed-sided travel crate that will do until your puppy grows out of it. If you don't have a travel crate, you will need a crate large enough for your dog to stand up and turn around in once she is full-grown, but no larger than that. If this seems too large for your still small puppy, place a box inside the crate to fill up some of the space. Too much room does not help house-training. The crate can be made of see-through wire mesh, or it can be a closed plastic box with wire mesh windows and door. It needs a solid floor; for some airline cages you may have to buy a floor plate (crate pan). Avoid flooring that is open mesh as you need a leakproof one. Line the crate with newspapers.

I would never try to house-train a puppy or a grown dog without a dog crate. It is the most humane thing you can give your dog, as dogs are den animals and the closed area represents safety and security. It is her own private space to go to when she wants to be alone, where no one will interrupt her peace and quiet. A crate is the fastest and easiest method of house-training, as dogs instinctively make every effort to keep their dens and sleeping places clean. The crate is also your protection against your puppy teething on electric wires (and possibly dying of it) or your best shoes, or eating the couch while you're not home. It's a place for time out during training and after misdemeanors.

Get your puppy used to her crate as soon as you bring her home and after she has had the opportunity to relieve herself outdoors. Let her investigate the open box, place a treat inside it or feed her there, then close the door and let her rest. She may initially fuss. Ignore her cries; they will stop in a few minutes, and soon she will be asleep. A puppy is not to be left crated for more than two hours at a time without being let out for a walk, feeding, petting, exercise, or play. If you work a day job, however, she may have to stay there longer. A pet sitter or friend who can come in every two or four hours for the first few months will help house-training tremendously.

To accustom an older dog to the crate who has never used one before takes a slightly longer process. Let the dog investigate the crate, feed her in it, place her bedding or a toy in it, and play with her there—all initially with the crate door open. Once the dog becomes tired, lure her into the box with a biscuit and shut the door for just a moment. At first sign of restlessness, let her out again. Try this a few times, initially staying with her while the door is closed. Then move away from her, but let her out within a few minutes. Gradually get her used to the crate for longer periods. With a new dog, until you know her habits and whether she is destructive or fully house-trained, make almost as much use of the crate as you would with a puppy. When you are not there to watch her, she should be in the crate.

Among other necessary tools and items, you will also need a bowl for food and one for water. These should be unbreakable, especially for puppies, and heavy enough not to move around while the dog or pup is eating and drinking. Stainless steel bowls are probably best for puppies, as they cannot be chewed up—puppies chew on everything. Never use aluminum bowls, which are toxic. A small puppy needs only small bowls; you can buy larger ones as she grows. A too large bowl invites feet in the food and playing in the water. Kali loved to do that and made a perpetual sloppy mess. She paddled in the water bowl, splashed in it, put bits of dog kibble in it to float and chase after, and dunked her tennis balls and stuffed toys in it. When the toys were thoroughly saturated and dripping, she liked to swing them around the house.

Place the food and water bowls on a washable cloth placemat or small area rug to catch and absorb the spills. For times when your pet stays in her crate, you may also wish to attach a rabbit watering bottle to it. Other than at night, your puppy should have clean, preferably filtered, water available to her at all times. She will eat up to four times a day. (Nutrition is discussed in a later chapter. For now, the key phrase in dog or puppy food is *preservative free*.) Plan to have a supply of food available and bowls ready by the time you bring your puppy or dog home.

A collar and leash are next. Buy a flat, webbed cloth or leather collar that buckles or one that closes with a seat belt snap. Do this whether your new dog is a puppy or grown. Also purchase a six-foot leash to match; for a puppy choose a very lightweight one. If your dog is an adult you may also wish to purchase a stainless steel training collar (a choke chain) but only for a dog over six months of age. The training collar fits if two to three inches of chain remain when the collar is tightened on the dog's neck. The flat-buckle collar fits if you can place two fingers between it and your dog's neck—no more, no less. For puppies, check the collar weekly for size, as puppies grow quickly. Some seat belt–type collars are adjustable.

The flat leather or webbed collar remains on the dog at all times. You will attach a name tag and later the dog's city license to it. The chain collar is used only for training and is not left on the dog unsupervised in the house, yard, or in her crate. It may catch on something and strangle her. ID tags with your name, address, phone number, and the dog's name are available from many sources. Check your veterinarian's office, pet shop, or any dog magazine. They are quite inexpensive and can bring your dog home if she bolts away from you or escapes from her yard. More permanent identification may be obtained by tattooing or micro-chipping. The companies that offer these services have national pet registries and your dog wears a numbered tag with instructions on her collar at all times. Each time you move, you must register your new address and phone number with the registry service. See your veterinarian for these options.

To get a puppy used to her flat collar, place it on her in a play session then praise her. Let her wear it for awhile, then take it off, praise her again, and in a few minutes put it on again. Take it on and off a few times and do this a couple of times a day for a week. If she struggles, distract her with a toy or an occasional tidbit. Most dogs get used to wearing a collar within a few minutes. The chain collar is not for use on small puppies; it is only for adults and only for obedience training. Leash training is discussed in a later chapter.

Other important puppy supplies are a liquid or foam enzymatic cleaner for urine stains, a baby gate to keep your puppy confined to one room, and a feces scooper for your yard or walks. If you have a puppy, accidents are inevitable. An enzymatic cleaner removes the odors that cause a dog to return to the same spot to do the deed again. Soap and water are not enough, as they remove only the odors we can smell—a dog's nose is far keener. The cleaner removes pet stains and keeps them from damaging your rugs, and is also effective on odors and stains from blood and vomit.

The gate keeps your puppy close to you so that when she is out of her crate you can watch her actions and take her outside quickly when needed. With a stern "no," she can be trained not to rush at, push, chew on, or climb over the gate. It's a valuable lesson: this early training will continue to apply to any gate. A two-handled scooper makes the necessary outdoor clean-up job easy. You do not have to bend, your target is easily grabbed and removed, and your hands are not dirty. Most city laws also require you to clean up after your dog if she defecates on the street or sidewalk. The scooper makes the job quick and simple.

To keep your puppy or dog clean and sweet, you will need some grooming tools. For a small puppy, a steel comb and soft bristled brush are enough. As she gets older, choose the tools best fitted to her breed and type of coat; ask a groomer or pet store clerk for advice. You will also need a toenail trimmer and styptic powder. For a puppy, your own fingernail clipper is probably enough to start; you will need a larger clipper later on unless your dog is very small. The styptic powder, called Kwik-Stop, halts bleeding if you hit the blood vessel in the nail while cutting it. This is not to scare you off from trimming nails, but to begin to teach you the process that continues in a later chapter.

If your dog has a coat that mats, you may wish to invest in a mat splitter. This is a comb-like tool that splits hair mats by cutting through them without pulling the dog's hair. Prevention is better than the cure in this case. Rather than resorting to a mat splitter, groom your dog often enough that mats don't develop to begin with. You may also wish to invest in a flea comb. This is a usually very fine toothed stainless steel comb; when you pull it through the dog's hair, the fleas remain on the comb to be killed by dropping them in soapy water. A quick-shedding blade will help you later with heavy shedders.

You will need toys for play and teething. Choose some toys that will not break into shreds or fragments when chewed. Only a couple are needed. A puppy is not to be left alone with plastic squeaky toys; she can tear them apart and swallow pieces that may choke her or obstruct her intestines. One squeaky toy small enough to hold in your palm is useful for training, however; you will handle it and she will play with it under supervision. A clean plastic soda bottle is fun to chase; remove the cap. Nylabones or Kong toys are great for teething puppies and all dogs like tennis balls. You may wish to have a rawhide bone or two available for teething, and also to keep your puppy occupied in her crate. Avoid beef hooves, as some dogs can swallow them whole, with choking or impacted bowels as a result. Personally, the idea of these disturbs me, as does that of pig ears—I have been a committed vegetarian for too long.

Some dogs love stuffed toys but understand that your puppy will destroy them and make a mess with the stuffing in the process. Remove plastic eyes and other trims that could be swallowed before giving them to her and make sure they are fully washable. Synthetic fleece stuffed toys found in pet shops are very sturdy and wear quite well for my dogs. Tiger had a pink fleece pillow that managed to survive her puppyhood; she slept with her head on it and never wet it or chewed it up. Your dog as well will have her likes and dislikes.

For grown dogs try tennis balls and synthetic fleece toys; adults are also less likely to swallow pieces from plastic squeaky things. Rawhide bones are a big hit but some dogs become too possessive of them, as Copper does. Your dog may snap or growl if approached while chewing on them. Instruct your children not to try to take toys or bones away from older dogs. With puppies you can occasionally take a toy away; but be sure to praise the dog, then give it back. Do this also with food. This will teach her that you are boss, but a nice one who returns things. It also teaches her to react in a safe way if a child interrupts her dinner or a game, or takes away one of her toys.

Helping Your Dog Adapt to New Surroundings

You now have your puppy and her supplies; what comes next? Bring the crate into the kitchen and set it up in a convenient place that will be its permanent location. Walk the puppy, feed her if she hasn't eaten in a couple of hours, give her a chance again to eliminate outdoors, then place her in her crate for an hour's sleep. Let her cry if she must; she will get used to the crate quickly. Don't scold her or go to her if she fusses or whines, just ignore her. Your puppy needs some space and so do you. Keep children away from her while she sleeps and let them know that the crate is the puppy's house and she is not to be disturbed there. When she wakes, take her outside again, play with her in the kitchen for a while, then put her back in her crate for another hour. She can watch you as you move around the kitchen. Placing the crate there gives the dog full view of the family's activities and makes her a part of them.

When she wakes the second time, she goes outside again, has another fifteen minutes or so play session and then it's probably time for a meal. A puppy under three months eats four times a day; from four to six months, three times; from six months to a year and a half, twice a day. Your adult dog is usually fed once a day in the morning or evening. This is the basic routine for a small puppy—wake, eliminate, eat, eliminate again, play, and nap. As she gets older her waking time will be longer, as will her time out of her crate. Remember that the crate is a place of rest and refuge where she may sleep or play, undisturbed and protected. It also keeps her out of mischief and makes house-training a breeze.

If your new dog is an adult, begin to get her used to being in the crate, but do not force the issue immediately. She will be in it far less than a puppy but you will want to crate her when you go out, at least until you know her habits and know that she can be trusted. As soon as you bring your grown dog home, give her a chance to eliminate outdoors. Then bring her in, and let her walk around in your home to sniff at all the new smells. Have the people in the family sit quietly, letting the dog approach them as she wishes to. Show her where her water bowl is and make sure it is filled, and show her the crate. Show the dog her yard, if you have one, and take her on leash to eliminate in the same place for the first several times. You may wish to leave a piece of her feces on the ground to bring her back to the spot you wish her to use. When the dog lies down to rest, do not disturb her. When she wakes, take her outside again to the spot you wish her to use for eliminating.

Whether your dog is a puppy or grown, you will wish to follow and supervise her activities closely, an adult dog for at least the first couple weeks, and a puppy until she is almost grown. There is no getting around it: raising a puppy is a full-time job for the first few months. Begin gentle pre-obedience training after a few days, starting out with a collar and leash for a puppy or getting her to follow you in the yard. With an older dog, training is more a process of discovering who she is, what she already knows, and what her habits and behavior patterns are. Formal obedience training should not begin with a new adult dog until she is comfortable and relaxed in her new home. Give it at least a couple of weeks or a month. With a puppy your first priority is house-training, but other learning that is not formal training is happening at the same time.

The first night with a new dog or puppy is probably your most stressful time and the dog's too. The new puppy has just been taken from her mother and litter mates and when it's quiet and dark she will miss them the most. To help her as much as you can, move her crate into your bedroom and place it beside your bed. If she wakes in the night and cries, take her out to eliminate (even at 2 AM) then put her back in the crate. If she cries again before another two hours go by, ignore it. Do not respond in any way. To do so encourages more crying. Don't expect to sleep much the first few nights, but your puppy will adjust. She will accept you as her new pack, attach to you, and gradually forget her canine mother.

Do the same for a new adult dog by placing her in her crate near your bed. If she will not accept the crate as yet, confine her to the room by closing the door and keep an ear out for her activities. Give her a rawhide bone to chew on. You may also temporarily use her leash to tie her to a piece of furniture in the bedroom. You want to keep both a puppy or grown dog confined until you know that they will behave. You cannot give a puppy freedom until she is reliably house-trained and is through teething. For an adult dog, unless she proves destructive, freedom may be granted quickly, within a couple of weeks. Whether crated or not on the first night, it is still important to train your grown dog to accept the crate. You may wish to do it gradually. At some point you will simply have to close the door and let her stay there a while, whether she fusses or not.

It is best to not bring either puppy or grown dog into bed with you, though it may be tempting. If you relent and do it the crying will stop and you may get a little sleep. You may also get peed on. By allowing it, you also set a precedent that elevates your dog to a family-pack status equal to yours, and this is a bad precedent. In a dog pack, the animal that sleeps in the highest spot is the recognized leader and boss. It is extremely important that you don't give messages to your new dog or puppy that she is boss, as she will take this seriously even at eight weeks old. *You* are her boss, hopefully a kind and motherly one, but boss all the same. If you share your bed with your puppy, at around six months of age she will decide that since she's been sleeping up high on your bed she must be *your* boss. It's an expected thought for a doggy teenager and you may have hard work convincing her otherwise. Keep your dog sleeping on the floor.

However, as your pup matures and older dog settles in, you may sometimes invite her to join you on the bed. Invite is the key here, you invite her or she doesn't come up. And when you say "off," her little paws must hit the floor. As the giver of invitations and commands you are still the boss and can have a warm puppy beside you when you wish it. By this time your baby is house-trained and you know and understand your grown dog and how much to trust her.

Choosing an Appropriate Name

On your dog's first day at home begin to think of a name. A name is important and you may take a few days to think of the best one for your puppy. An adult dog may come to you already named and if she answers to it you will not want to change it. If your puppy is purebred and not previously AKC registered, you will need to give her two names, a short one to call her by (that is her real name), and a formal registration name that can be longer. The best call name is one or two syllables long, easy to say. It should not embarrass you when you use it in public and it should not sound like an obedience command.

Respect your dog's dignity when choosing a name. A sugary name like Baby or Darling may work for an infant but not once your baby reaches eighty pounds. A name like Killer or Maniac is inappropriate and a negative invitation for your dog to live up to. Likewise, avoid derogatory terms as a name, like Stupid or Lazy, and profane ones like Damn You; they are not fair to the innate dignity of any dog. The most basic obedience commands are Sit, Down, Stay, Heel, and Come, with No also an obedience direction. Avoid giving your dog a name that sounds like one of these, it will only confuse her later. If you wish to show your dog in obedience competition, you cannot change the standard commands that every dog is trained to respond to. Sitka sounds too much like Sit, May or Ray sounds like Stay, and Yoyo sounds too much like No.

Think carefully about your puppy's name before you finally decide. Names are words of power. This might be a good time to begin inter-species communication with your dog or puppy. Ask her what her real name is or what she might like to be called. Copper named himself as soon as I took him from the animal shelter. Kali decided that though she is a reincarnation of Dusty, she did not want to be called Dusty this time. She also doesn't like to be compared to Dusty. I asked if she liked the name Pat gave her and she did, and so she is Kali. Pets tend to live up to their names, so if you name your dog for a destroyer Goddess (as I did with Kali) you may get what you asked for.

A puppy may be able to tell you what she was called in her most recent past life. She may also be too young, too much an infant to communicate with. A grown dog may not be ready to talk with you right away, especially if she is in trauma over losing a former home or being in a shelter, or if she has been abused. You will have to gain her trust first. You will have to make the final choice of a name. Once you have picked it, ask your dog or puppy if she approves. Her agreement will make it easier and faster to teach her to respond. You will have more cooperation from the start. If she strongly objects, think seriously about picking another name.

It's probably inevitable that you will use a nickname, or several nicknames for your puppy or dog. Tiger was Grubby, Dusty was Greedy Girl and Wildness, Copper is the Moose, and Kali is Missy Stars when she is not being Missy Mess. Such names are not used in training or in obedience commands but may be used in play. It's best not to teach your pup to respond to nicknames as they will confuse her. Teach her to respond only to her call name; when she hears it she learns to pay attention. When she hears a nickname, she knows it's a game. Most nicknames are not for public use. However, even with these silly names, avoid those that denigrate the animal's dignity.

While the first few days and nights with a new puppy or dog are stressful, your newest family member will settle in quickly. The all-night crying will stop within a few nights and puppy house-training will take only a couple of months if you are consistent doing it. In a short time, your dog will move into your home and heart to reside there for the rest of her life. A little discomfort, a little work, and the lack of sleep are worth it to gain the love she will bring you for the next many years. Treat your new puppy or dog gently and quietly from the beginning and her training will be easy and her life a happy one. Remember that she has a soul as large as yours. She is an intelligent "Great Intergalactic Be-ing," and she is made of love.

settling in—house-training and socialization

The first order of business for a new dog or puppy is house-training, the second is socialization, and the third is teaching her to accept handling and grooming. All three are essential. They will become the most important lessons in family-pack living that your pet must learn. For puppies, these priorities are obvious (a baby has never been taught), but they are also important and necessary for a grown dog.

The adult dog you bring home may not be house-trained. She may have never lived indoors if she was a kennel dog or racetrack rescue. She may not recognize your home as her territory and therefore may not understand that she must not soil it. She may be so traumatized that she forgets whatever she once knew about indoor behavior. While the house-training schedule is looser for an older dog—she doesn't need to go out as often since her body is mature—the process of house-training is much the same for an adult as for a puppy.

Socialization is the next major priority, especially for a new pup. The training may also be needed for a grown dog. The grown dogs that need it often need it badly. Socialization means getting an animal used to all kinds of people and places, thus making it possible for her to go with you anywhere. She may react with caution to new situations or people but not with fear or aggression. The dog that runs and hides when visitors come was not properly socialized as a puppy. Your pet must be taught to approach all humans with respect and threaten no one—not the mail carrier with her strange bag, the delivery person that comes to the door, the person she meets on a walk, people on bicycles, the vet, or anyone you welcome into your house or yard. Both dog and puppy must learn to ride quietly in a car, to behave in other people's homes, and to react safely to strangers and children who approach or pet her.

Likewise, your puppy or dog has to accept being handled. You must be able to clip her toenails, brush and groom her, bathe her, and clean her ears and anal glands. If she is a breed that requires professional clipping, she must accept the process quietly. The dog must allow a veterinarian to handle her and accept being medicated internally and externally by you or by your vet. These good manners are much easier to train in a puppy than in an adult dog that has never been handled. A puppy who is not trained for these processes becomes a terror and a trial as an adult and may even be in danger if you cannot medicate or handle her.

The Importance of Timing and Schedules

Though all three basics are taught simultaneously, let's start with house-training. (Grooming is in the next chapter.) This is the one that keeps most pet guardians anxious for the first several months with their new puppy. The previous chapter's sequence of events for the first day home is continued every day, and is the basis for house-training both puppies and full-grown dogs. Dogs physiologically, psychologically, and instinctively need structure and a daily schedule. They have strong internal clocks and they depend upon predictable events in their lives— if it's 10 AM it's walk time. When a daily schedule of feeding, eliminating, play, and sleep is adhered to, their bodies and minds fall into the structure and they welcome it. It represents order and security. By keeping your pet on an unchanging schedule, you will know when she needs to eliminate and have her at the acceptable place every time (or at least most of the time).

As soon as you wake up, take the puppy from her crate and carry her outdoors to the place you have chosen for her elimination. Even if you have a fenced-in yard, put the puppy on a leash and carry her to the spot. Pick a phrase to mean elimination, one that you will use all the time and that the pup will learn to connect with the act. "Hurry up," or "Let's do it" might be some choices. The phrase should not be embarrassing if others hear it, and should not resemble any obedience direction. Eventually, your pup will eliminate on command, so choose a phrase that you won't use for other things. Stand quietly with the puppy or dog until she accomplishes her mission. This is not play time; don't talk to her other than to say her phrase. When she does the job, praise her quietly in a high, bright voice. Wait a few minutes to be sure she's really done, then take her in the house. She can walk back in herself or you may carry her. Take her to the same spot every time. You may wish to leave a piece of feces on the ground; the odor will induce her to eliminate there again.

Now feed your puppy and clean up her crate while she's eating. Take soiled newspapers out of the house so their scent will also be out of your home. After mopping up, use your enzymatic odor eliminator to wipe out the crate and spread new newspapers. Please note that I do not recommend paper-training your puppy. Train her to defecate outdoors, so you will not have to train her twice. Some people with tiny breeds train them to use a litter box. If so, the dog should also be trained outdoors; you may place some litter on her spot outside. Even in winter in cold climates it is safe to take your puppy out unless the freeze is an extremely severe one. Puppies are sturdier than they look and she will not be outdoors long.

For an adult dog, put her on a leash and walk her to the place you have chosen outdoors. Walk her back and forth a few feet but again this is work and not playtime so do it quietly and matter of factly. Use your command of "Hurry up" or "Let's do it." Praise your dog thoroughly when she is finished, make sure she is truly finished, and bring her back inside. For her first time out in the morning your dog or puppy may need to urinate and/or eliminate more than once. Make sure she is finished before returning home. Older male dogs can seldom resist marking bushes; walk him back and forth and praise him for the inevitable. He will need to do it a number of times before he is satisfied. Better your bushes than your furniture.

After your puppy eats, play quietly with her for a few minutes, then take her out again. She will need to eliminate again about fifteen minutes after eating. You may put her in her crate and use the fifteen minutes to get dressed or tend to your own needs. Then take her out again, as you did before. Grown dogs can hold it longer but I find that mine want to go out both before and after meals. Once your pet is trained, you can simply open the door and send her outside if you have a fenced yard. Until she is fully trained, however, take her on a leash and make sure she really goes.

Bring your puppy in, then put her in her crate and let her nap. Do not rough-house with a dog or puppy after eating. Some large dog breeds are subject to bloat (gastric torsion-life threatening, acute indigestion). Keeping quiet after eating is a good prevention for bloat and also prevents simpler stomach upsets and spitting up. A dog will naturally choose to rest after eating and should be encouraged to do so. When she wakes, whether adult or puppy, take her outside immediately to eliminate again. Now begin a playtime and let her investigate your kitchen or yard a while. A young puppy that eats four times a day will almost be ready for another meal by this time and the routine starts again.

You will learn to recognize when your puppy needs to go out. She needs a walk immediately upon waking, a few minutes after eating, at the end of play-time or any excitement, and the last thing at night. If her nose goes to the ground and she starts sniffing and circling, pick her up immediately and take her out. This will mean taking walks about every hour and a half for a small pup and gradually increasing the intervals between the walks. A grown dog is good for several hours but a newcomer should go out about every three hours at first. Her time between walks will extend also, and an adult dog will stay clean in her crate as long as necessary. A puppy physiologically cannot do this and should not be expected to. The trick to house-training any dog or puppy is to keep her on a strict schedule of feeding and walks and to anticipate (using that schedule) when she will need to be taken outside. Keeping the schedule strictly is impor-tant at the beginning; once the puppy or dog is reliable and can physically wait, you can relax somewhat.

What about mistakes? They are inevitable, of course, and they are not shameful or tragic but part of the natural process. You will praise your puppy or dog every time she eliminates outdoors but you will *never* hit her or rub her nose in it when she errs. In this case, your first move is to take her out to her acceptable spot. Pick her up and carry her there. Do not scold or speak, just take her outside, use her elimination phrase, and praise her in the right place.

Some trainers feel that your puppy should not watch you clean up her mistakes. Perhaps someone else in the house could do this while you take the pup outside or you could leave her in the yard alone for a moment while you do the clean up. Perhaps neither is practical, so just take the puppy out immediately and then clean up the mess indoors. If you are using the baby gate and crate, these errors will not cause damage and are quick to clean up.

Again, I must repeat: you will *never* hit a puppy or rub her nose in her mistakes. Once she begins to understand what you want of her, usually around four months, you may speak a sharp and low-pitched, growling "no" as you grab her up and head for the yard. Do not shout—her hearing is much better than yours, and shouting will only frighten her needlessly. With an adult dog, your "no" can be more urgent, sharper and louder—she knows she's doing wrong. You may be able to stop her in the act. Then hustle her outside immediately. A grown dog can house-train in as quickly as a week but may need to continue on the schedule longer. A puppy has little physiological ability to hold her eliminations until she reaches four months. Do not expect her to start being reliable before six months. The schedule lengthens as the puppy gets older; a six-month-old puppy can usually wait three hours for her walk, as long as she goes out before and after meals.

Your puppy's last meal of the day should not be later than 8 PM for a young puppy. When she reaches four months, the evening meal should be discontinued. An adult dog can have her daily meal either in the morning or at dinnertime. Leaving her a few hours between the last feeding and bedtime allows your pet the chance to stay drier at night in her crate. You may pick up the water bowl after 8 PM for a puppy but I recommend leaving her the rabbit bottle (not much water comes out of it) longer. Walks continue all through the day and evening, with one last trip outside just before your bedtime. Then place the puppy in her crate in your bedroom for the night. Also keep the grown dog near you so you know if she gets restless to go out.

Sometimes staying dry through the night happens early but for some puppies it's the last step. Tiger did not stop wetting at night until I let her stay out of her crate. She took to house-training quickly; by eight weeks of age, she was sitting at the door when she needed to go out. If I didn't see her there, I cleaned up the consequences, but she truly tried and she understood the routine much younger than any other of my pups. At six months, however, she was still wetting her crate at night and fussing and crying on most nights. I didn't want to let her out but the noise had to stop. I finally decided to try her out of the crate at night and used her leash to tie her to the bedroom dresser. She stayed dry without fussing about it and the leash came off, too. She was already keeping clean in her crate while I went to work, so I knew she could physically hold it.

House-training is hardest if no one is home all day to take the puppy out on schedule but it can be done. It will probably take longer. Keep to the frequent walk schedule on evenings and weekends and the crate is an absolute necessity in this circumstance. Your puppy will stay clean in her crate for as long as she can and start staying dry all day sooner than you may expect. As soon as you come home take her out. Use lots of praise when she goes outdoors but ignore the wets and messes in the crate. Any time you come home to a dry puppy, praise her effusively and rush her outside immediately.

Eventually, your dog will tell you when she needs to go. She may sit by the door, come to you and lick your hand (as Kali does), or pace back and forth in front of you (Copper). A fenced yard becomes a real blessing here, as by this time you no longer need the leash, but need only open the back door. It is crucial to never let your dog run free for eliminating or anything else. If you don't have a fenced yard you must use a leash. Dogs die rapidly in traffic, they may run off and not know how to come home again, and they can also be stolen or picked up by animal control officers. During early house-training, take your dog out on her leash even in a fenced yard. Once she understands what she is there for, you can let her loose in your yard, but in your fenced-in secure yard only.

Dog or Puppy Socialization

While your puppy is being toilet trained, she must also be trained for socialization. To wait until later will be too late, as the socialization must occur during key developmental periods in a puppy's life, most of which occur when she is very young. As soon as her first immunizations are given, you can begin the socialization with people and places. Wait until after her second immunizations before introducing her to other animals, unless you know that they are healthy and immunized. Don't allow a young puppy to sniff the feces of other dogs not in her household. (A fuller discussion on immunization comes in a later chapter.) Your puppy may be at some small risk for picking up dis-ease when you take her out of your home environment but the consequences and risk are greater if she has not been socialized thoroughly and socialized as young as possible.

An unsocialized dog is afraid or resentful of anything new that enters her environment. She may run and hide when people come to visit, she may quiver in terror in a new place and urinate on the floor, and she may be impossible for a veterinarian to handle. If you take her for a walk and other people or dogs approach, she may quiver, scream, try to hide or run away, or come out snarling and biting. She may feel so threatened that she has to attack and bite people or another dog. She refuses to make friends. An unsocialized dog may bite the mail carrier and the post office may refuse to deliver your mail. Taken in the car, she may run back and forth and may cause an accident. You can't take her with you traveling, visiting, or anywhere else, because when you do, the dog becomes hysterical, terrified, defensive, or aggressive, or acts as if she had never been house-trained.

This isn't what you want for your puppy and the whole syndrome is easy to prevent from the start. It is unfortunately harder but possible to cure in adult dogs. Socialization simply means taking your puppy or dog out in public and getting her used to the world. In her crate, take her for short car rides—before a meal rather than after to prevent car-sickness. If she rides in her crate every time, she is safely confined and will cause no accidents as she learns that cars are fun. Doing this routinely when she is a puppy will generally mean you don't need a crate in the car when she gets older. If it does not, keep a crate in your car, or invest in a pet seat belt system available from dog suppliers. Talk to her calmly and praise her when she is in the crate, praise her again when you arrive, and let her out of the crate on her leash. Use the automobile trips to take you to other sites for socialization training.

My favorite place for puppy socialization is the supermarket. Stand outside a busy store with a puppy in your arms and you will receive lots of attention. Tell people, "You can pet her," and your pup will meet lots of new and friendly strangers in a half hour's time. If she shrinks from the attention, hold her, and let it continue anyway. Do not comfort her and praise her only when she is allowing someone to touch her without flinching. Offering comfort only encourages the shyness and tells her there is something to worry about. Do this for half an hour every few days and the shyness will end after two or three sessions. As she gets older and bolder, stop holding her and let her walk on leash.

It is important that your puppy gets to know all sorts of people. We may think people are all alike but a dog doesn't see it that way. She needs to be petted by men and women, children of varying ages including infants, the elderly, and people of all colors. She needs to see and be petted by people carrying packages, which she will think is part of their body shape and may frighten her. She needs to meet the mail carrier and any regular delivery people or meter-readers. The mail carrier in my neighborhood brings biscuits in his pockets and all the dogs love him. It is important that the puppy meet only friendly people, too. If someone is hostile to dogs or may be rough or hurt her, keep the pup away. All her encounters with humans need to be positive ones.

Places are next. Take your puppy with you everywhere you can. Walk her on your street and on other streets, always on leash. Walk her near traffic and through crowds. Take her to the laundromat and through the carwash in your car. Take her to stores and to other people's houses. Allow her to meet and get to know other dogs, cats, small animals, and small children. Keep her on her leash so that you can supervise these meetings, and if all is well let her play with the animals or children. A dog that refuses to approach other dogs without a fight does so because she hasn't seen a dog since she left her litter. Dogs are social creatures and to isolate them this way is unkind and against all canine instinct.

Take socialization training trips at least twice a week and make them a priority until your puppy is at least six months old. Puppies pass through two distinct fear phases in their early development that you will see, the first at about eight weeks of age and the second at about four months. In these periods she will seem shyer and flightier than usual. Continue the socialization but make it very gentle. The fear periods end in a week or so. Do not stop socializing her because she seems afraid of her own shadow at this time. Half an hour at a time of visiting new places, being petted by strangers, or meeting other dogs and cats is enough, but do it often, twice a week or more. Rides in the car need only be a few minutes to begin with.

A wonderful help with puppy socialization is KPT, Kindergarten Puppy Training, available through dog obedience schools. While mostly for purebred pups, classes for mixed-breeds are also available from obedience schools or from your Humane Society or animal shelter. This series of pre-obedience classes is usually open to puppies from four to six months old. Preliminary obedience is taught as play and puppies get to meet each other and other people in a strange new setting. The teacher can help you with any problems in behavior or house-training you may be having with your pet and the early training makes real obedience later a breeze. The weekly support and idea sharing with other puppy guardians is welcome and useful, too, and KPT is fun for all concerned. Start your puppy in it as soon as she is old enough for a class, the earlier the better.

Another good socialization venue, if only for purebreds, is the dog club–sponsored AKC Puppy Match. Whether you plan on showing your dog or not, the Matches are open to any AKC registered puppy and are great fun for both dogs and people. A Puppy Match may be limited to one breed only or open to all breeds (an All-Breed Match). They are run like professional dog shows and you will want to do

Age	Period	Development	What to Do
0–2 wks.	Newborn	Sleeps, suckles	
2–3 wks.	Transitional	Senses begin to operate	Gentle handling
3–12 wks.	Socialization		
3–5 wks.	1st stage	React to loud sounds.	Give separate sleep and play areas, provide complex environment, plenty of human contact and contact with other dogs.
5–8 wks.	2nd stage	Weaning begins. Hierarchy games played in litter.	Socialization continues. Puppies leave for new home.
8–12 wks.	3rd stage	Independent exploratory behavior, begins assessment of position in pack.	Socialization continues. Puppy learns to play human games and learns about position in the pack.
3–6 mos.	Juvenile	Explores farther afield. Chewing is a priority.	Training and good manners are developed. Low status impressed on puppy. Socialization increases.
6–12/18 mos.	Adolescence	More independent. Sexual maturity reached. Territorial behavior begins.	Difficult time for owners. Continue with training: watch out for challenges to authority.
12/18 mos. onward			Relax and enjoy a well-balanced dog.

1 Gwen Bailey, *The Perfect Puppy: How to Raise a Well-Behaved Dog,* (Pleasantville, NY, Reader's Digest, 1995), p. 40.

some preliminary reading on dog show procedures before attending. A Match's puppy classes are divided by age. You and your pup go into the show ring with other puppies of her breed, age, and sex. She must be able to walk reasonably on a leash and accept physical handling from the judge of the class. The puppies are trotted around the ring together and separately. The judge will examine each pup, running her hands along the dog's body, looking at her teeth, and checking a male dog's testicles. She names a winner, second, third, and fourth for each class and winners compete with the first place dogs of other classes.

Your actual time in the show ring is only a few minutes, but bring your puppy's crate with you, as it can be a long day. When you are not in the ring, there are other dogs to meet and people to talk shop with. I especially enjoy the vendors' booths at dog shows and matches, with their leashes and grooming supplies, books, and the tee-shirts and other objects that picture your breed. If your puppy proves competitive for conformation showing, you may want to try professional dog shows later. The youngest your puppy may be to do that is six months. Most dogs totally enjoy Puppy Matches and shows and people get infected by the show bug very easily. For information on Puppy Matches, ask your puppy's breeder or write to the AKC (see Resources) for information on Matches and dog breed clubs in your area. You may wish to join a Purebred Dog Club as well.

An adult dog that comes to you unsocialized may be difficult to change or heal. If she has been abused it may not be fully possible. Start with an adult dog by taking her for rides, again in her crate. If she has difficulty, keep the rides short but continue them, offering lots of praise. The crate is necessary for both puppies and adults but the car may be less of a problem than her fear of people.

A very shy or fear-aggressive adult dog should not be petted by all comers. Instead, bring a quiet new person into your home. Let the dog come up to her in her own time as the person sits on the floor at the dog's level. If the dog does not come by herself, you may have to lead her to the visitor; put her on leash to do this. After the dog has investigated the person, she may talk softly to the dog and pet her if the dog allows it. Do this with lot of different people, indoors and one at a time.

Once the pet relaxes, try the same procedure outdoors on a leash. The new person walks up, then crouches down to dog level. She lets the animal come to her and pets the dog if she is permitted to do so by the dog. The process may be slow. The person must keep her hands down and quiet, as formerly abused dogs are hand-shy. She may interpret sudden hand movements as the person preparing to hit her.

Once your dog is willing to let people approach, start walking her in many different environments. Walk on both quiet streets and noisy streets; go to parks and outdoor fairs if your dog is not aggressive. Keep her on leash and close to you at all times and do not allow people to approach her if she is stressed or could be unsafe. If she meets other animals, let it be on neutral territory (not at home or in either dog's yard), and keep her on leash until you are sure of her reaction. I do not advise introducing an adult dog to cats or small animals. If you try it, the new animal should be in a crate or cage for its protection. As the dog sees more people and places, and learns that she will not be beaten or abused, her social abilities will gradually improve. If she has been badly abused or abused for long, however, change may happen only very slowly and some behaviors will not heal.

Once your grown dog is manageable in strange places and non-threatening to other dogs, try an obedience class. Whether she has already been trained or not is unimportant; the purpose of the class is socialization. Obedience training builds confidence and can be used for a variety of problems, even when the problem is not actually obedience. A private dog trainer or animal behaviorist can also work wonders with formerly abused dogs and can offer answers and techniques in or out of formal class. When choosing a trainer or obedience class watch the person work before bringing your dog to her. You want a trainer who is gentle, who works with compassion, and has animal savvy, rather than one who works with brute force.

The most important socialization you can offer your puppy or dog begins at home. Stroke, touch, and cuddle her often, offering constant reassurance and praise. Treat her always with gentleness. Never intimidate her or frighten her with over-correction or rough treatment. Be watchful of children to see that they act gently at all times, and protect the puppy from rough acting adults or children anywhere. Keep playtimes quiet and easy and avoid yelling or rough-housing. A protected and unfrightened dog or puppy becomes a friendly and reliable pet. Fear is your worst enemy if you want your puppy to be well-mannered and safe when grown.

The third necessity for starting your puppy or dog off right is teaching her to allow grooming and handling. This is discussed in the next chapter.

handling and grooming

Both you and other people must be able to handle your puppy for a variety of purposes. Keeping a dog clean and healthy requires such handling. You and your veterinarian must be able to examine her. You will need to give her medication at times or dress a wound and if she is unmanageable your dog may suffer or have to be sedated to be treated. If you have a breed that requires professional grooming, the groomer must be able to do her job with minimal fuss and without danger. Whatever breed, you will want to do routine maintenance and grooming yourself—baths, toenail cutting, brushing, and cleaning ears and anal glands. A well-behaved dog will also allow you to clean her teeth, which can prevent infections and lengthen her life as she ages.

Puppy Matches provide good training for your dog in being handled. Show dogs learn early to accept bathing and brushing, trimming, grooming, and clipping. They are taught to stand still and accept these procedures and most dogs exposed to these early enjoy them. When Dusty was with me I could place her on her side and she would lie still while I brushed her, trimmed her toenails on that side, checked her teeth, and examined every inch of her body. She would complain a little but stayed still. When I told her to turn over, she would offer me her other side so I could complete the process.

Copper is just the opposite. He came to me as a young adult, whereas Dusty was with me from birth. Apparently Copper had never been trained to be handled. I can only brush him a few strokes before he bolts. When I have to medicate him or clean his ears he dodges away or hides his head under the bed. Toenails are an ordeal. No groomer will try it more than once and the vets want to sedate him before they'll consider it. It takes several people to hold him in order to trim his toenails. He screams as if he's being murdered and thrashes and bites. While the biting is only half-hearted, his shrieking scares most people off. Baths are another story—he likes them.

Kali was a different problem, despite being Dusty's reincarnation. She came to me half-grown and had probably never been handled or groomed. She is more manageable. I can cut her toenails and examine her, and she likes to take vitamins and remedies. But a grooming brush sends her into a rage and tantrums, when she tries to bite me. She may have been struck or abused with a grooming brush. My only solution is not ideal: food is all-important to Kali and while she's eating dinner I can usually brush her for a brief few minutes. She rages but lets me do it, as her food is more important than the brush which she hates. Once her dinner is finished, however, I have to move my hand quickly or she'll bite me. Some of her favorite other people can brush her a little. Like Copper, Kali enjoys baths and makes no fuss about them, whether done in a bathtub or with the hose outdoors.

While Kali and Copper came to me with handling phobias that I have not been able to change, your puppy can be more like Dusty if you start her early. If your dog comes to you as an adult, you may have problems similar to those I have with Kali and Copper. If your grown dog comes from a breeding kennel or a greyhound track, she will likely accept handling. If she has been neglected or abused, you may have difficulties, though most dogs like to be brushed. Nevertheless, your pet needs to be groomed and bathed, and if a muzzle or an assistant are required, you may have to use them. If you have just adopted an adult dog, it's best to get her used to you for a few days before you try to bathe or brush her. Let her ears and toenails wait longer or let your vet do them the first time.

Teaching Your Puppy to Accept Handling and Grooming

Let's start your puppy off right, teaching her to accept handling from the beginning. Spend a few minutes daily stroking her and touching every part of her body. Put her in a standing position on the floor or a table, and gently hold her there by placing one hand under her chest, behind her front legs. Stroke her all over, taking each paw and leg into your hand and rubbing it; touch all her toes and pads. Open her mouth by pulling back her lips and running your finger along her teeth. Stroke her ears and touch them gently outside and inside. Stroke her underside, genitals, and tail, all very gently. Praise her as you do this. Consider it petting her. It will feel very good to her.

Keep her standing until you are fully done and at the end of the session give her a tidbit—a piece of puppy kibble, dog biscuit, cheese or bit of meat; a quarter-inch piece is enough. Use the command word "stand" any time you hold her in the standing position to be touched and examined. Follow the session with some playtime. If your pup is on a table, always keep one hand on her. If the phone rings, carry her with you or put her on the floor. Never leave her on a table alone.

Once a week, hold her closely in your arms (later she will stand) while trimming her toenails with a human fingernail clipper. Be very careful to cut only the part of the nail that is hooked over and not to hit the vein or quick. If you cut the quick, the nail will bleed; use styptic powder to stanch it. Cutting the vein hurts, and your dog will remember it, so avoid this as much as possible. Trim the nails on only one paw in a session, speaking matter of factly as you work and praising her when you finish. Dogs are instinctively foot shy and some dogs never accept toenail cutting—but it's necessary to do it.

Years ago when I had a grooming shop, a man carried in a medium-sized older mixed-breed dog. He said she hadn't been able to walk for over a year because of arthritis but he wanted her nails cut. The dog's toenails were over two inches long. She made no objection to my cutting them and when it was done the dog got up and walked out of the shop.

In the dog, a vein runs down the center of each toenail. If the nail is white, you can see it as a pink spongy area, and if you see the vein you can avoid cutting it. If the nail is black, it is less easy to see. Shine a flashlight under the nail to give you an idea of where the quick is. With black nails, trim only what part of the nail that is hooked over, or trim in very small bits so you can stop at the first sign of bleeding. Don't forget to trim the dewclaws on the sides of the paws also. They are usually on the front legs and sometimes on the hind ones. Some breeders remove the dewclaws on their puppies, as they can catch on things and break. A broken dewclaw toe-bone becomes a serious bleeding problem. If the claw is to be removed it must be done when the puppy is only forty-eight hours old. Dogs use these extra toes and I have never seen a dewclaw accident but the nails need to be kept short to prevent them. These dewclaw nails tend to get long very quickly, as they are not worn off by running, and they need to be kept trimmed.

If you hit a vein while trimming nails, take a pinch of the styptic powder, made of sulfur and alum, and press it into the nail. The bleeding will stop in a few moments. Be matter of fact about this event, as it's fairly routine and your puppy will follow your reaction. You may wish to try toenail trimming with a file or a grinder, available from pet and grooming suppliers.

Copper has a few things to say about toenails. When I asked him why he wouldn't let me cut them, his reply was, "It's the law of the foot." "What's that?" I asked him. "It means don't touch my feet," was Copper's answer. I asked, "Why not?" "Dogs run," was his reply. I tried again: "Wouldn't they run better with trimmed toenails?" "No," he said and wouldn't talk about it any more.

Baths are another common maintenance routine. Dogs actually need them infrequently and mine go several months between baths. Brushing will keep your pet clean longer, so baths are usually done only if you find fleas or your puppy delights in mud puddles (as Kali does). You will bathe your dog no more than once a month, as soap and water are drying for her delicate skin. It is important, however, to get your puppy used to being bathed and a few extra baths when she is young helps in her training.

You can bathe your dog or puppy in a bathtub or sink, or in hot weather, outside with a garden hose. Place a collar and leash on your pet and tie the leash to something fixed in position. Fill a few inches of water in the bathtub or sink and have your tools ready before you bring your dog into the bath. Dogs that run and hide at the sound of a tub filling—they always know when it's for them—can be caught and tied before you begin. Move them into the tub when you are ready.

Bath Accessories and Techniques

Besides the collar and leash, you will need cotton balls, hydrogen peroxide, olive oil, soap, a plastic cup, washcloth, towels, hair dryer, and a brush. A flexible shower hose is a great help, too. The water for bathing should feel comfortably warm to you, as a dog's normal body temperature is three degrees hotter than that of humans. Cold-water bathing is the prime reason why many dogs hate baths. If you use warm but not hot water most will accept the process without a fuss. Begin by brushing your dog's coat thoroughly. Any snarls and tangles will mat solid when wet and must be removed before the bath.

Next dampen a cotton ball with peroxide and gently wipe out the inside of the puppy's ears. You may also use witch hazel, alcohol, white vinegar, or echinacea tincture for this. Go as far in as you can reach with the cotton ball but do not use cotton swabs. Then take another cotton ball or piece of one and put a little olive or other vegetable oil on it; leave this in the ear opening for the length of the bath to prevent water from entering the ear canal. If your puppy or dog's ears are sweet and pink, no more needs done. If the ears are inflamed, odorous, or have a discharge which may look like moist coffee grounds, she has an infection or ear mites. See your holistic veterinarian or look up the entry on ear infections in Chapter 10. Also see my book, *The Natural Remedy Book for Dogs and Cats*.

Now place your pet in the warm water, asking her to "stand." Use the plastic cup or shower hose to wet her coat, taking care not to get water in her eyes. Talk to her gently through the process. Next soap her up, starting with a ring of suds around her neck just behind her head. This will prevent any fleas present from moving to her face until the end of the bath and then returning. Use only a very mild soap; many commercial dog groomers use Ivory dishwashing liquid for bathing. If your dog is very dirty or has fleas use a blue dishwashing liquid. Expensive pet shampoos are unnecessary, and flea shampoos are toxic and also not necessary.

Soap up your pet up thoroughly from the head back, making sure the soap reaches her underside, groin, and armpit areas, as well as her tail and under it. Use a washcloth on her face, being careful not to get soap or water in her eyes. If she has fleas, let the soap remain on her body for ten minutes, staying with her at all times and keeping a hand on her. You may clear her anal glands at this time, if she is six months old or older. If she does not have fleas, clear the anal gland then begin to rinse.

Anal glands are a pair of pea-sized oil sacks located under the dog's tail in the lower part of the anal opening. If your dog suddenly develops body odor, begins biting at her hindquarters, or scoots her rump on the floor, she probably has an anal gland blockage. Raw sores on her back above the tail can also indicate an anal gland problem. Male dogs may have more difficulties with this than females. The gland is simple to empty once you get the knack of it and it is always done in the bath.

If you are right-handed, grasp your dog's tail and lift it with your left hand. With your right hand, using your thumb and index finger in a pinching motion, grasp the lower anal opening on both sides. Press in and down. A stream of foul-smelling brown fluid, liquid or pasty in texture, will squirt out. One expression of the gland is enough. If you do it quickly, it's over and done with before your dog has time to react. For any dog over six months, the gland should be checked and expressed with every bath. In some breeds, like Siberian Huskies however, the anal glands may be too far into the rectum to empty in this way. Your vet or groomer can do it if needed.

Now rinse your puppy or dog off thoroughly. This will take longer than the soaping up and it is very important that all the soap is removed. Feel her undersides, chest, groin, and her back above the tail. When you think your pet is soap-free, rinse once or twice more. Soap remaining in the dog's coat will cause an itchy skin, scratching, and even skin sores. When thoroughly rinsed, let your pup shake off. If you keep your hand on her head during the bath she won't shake and make you wetter than she is.

Wrap her in towels and rub her as dry as you can. Remove the cotton balls if they are still in place. You may use a hair dryer to complete the drying. Get her used to it the first few times by turning it on held away from her and letting her see and hear it before you bring it close. Blow it on a cool cycle and let the air touch her feet before you turn it on her body. Some dogs dislike a dryer but if you get her used to it she will probably accept it.

Keep your puppy warm and protected from chilling. Until she is completely dry keep her indoors. Otherwise doggy instinct will send her to roll in something smelly immediately after a bath and you don't want to do it again. Once she is dry or almost so, brush her again thoroughly. Doing this with a northern breed dog will fill several wastebaskets with clean soft fur. (If your dog is shedding, or a Siberian Husky, you may wish to put a drain screen on your bathtub for her bath.) If you use a hair dryer, do the brushing and grooming while the dryer is on her and the dog is almost dry. It makes a fluffy, lovely coat, especially for dogs like poodles, and is a dog groomers' secret. If you clip your dog yourself, you will do so before the bath and scissors and finish her coat after it.

Working with a Professional Groomer

Dogs whose breed requires clipping usually have their baths at the grooming shop. Choose a groomer by watching her work and visiting her establishment. The place should be clean, well equipped, the dogs reasonably quiet, and the groomer should show patience in handling animals. A good grooming shop contains gates and other measures to keep the dogs from escaping outdoors. Pick a groomer who works in public view—she is one that you can trust not to hit a misbehaving dog. Choose one whose work appeals to you: how do the dogs that are ready to go home look? Discuss with your groomer at what age to begin clipping your puppy. Most groomers take them very young, by twelve weeks, to get them used to the process gradually. Though puppies require very little clipping for their immature coats, it is important to get them used to baths, hair dryers, clippers, grooming, and being handled.

Tell your new groomer that your puppy has never been groomed before. She will then take special care to introduce the puppy to each step gently and to make it fun. If your grown dog is new to you, tell her that also. You will not know her reactions yet to being groomed, how she will behave, or if she is afraid of any of the procedures. If your puppy will "stand" on command, tell the groomer; your puppy will stand if you have used the word consistently when you handle her. She also needs to know if your dog is a show prospect. Some groomers do not do show clips and many people who show learn to groom their own breed. If you start your puppy early with a groomer who takes the time to accustom her to the process, you will have no difficulties. Most dogs enjoy being groomed. It's a day out with other dogs and an opportunity to receive lots of attention.

Dental Care

As part of her grooming at home you may wish to teach your pup to accept tooth cleaning. This seems frivolous but an older dog can develop decay and infections that spread systemic dis-ease through her body. Such infections can shorten the life of an elderly dog. You also know that tooth cavities are painful and uncomfortable. While you cannot repair cavities yourself and few vets will do it, tooth cleaning can help to prevent them. Vitamin C is crucial for both dogs and people in preventing tooth decay, too. You will read more about vitamins in a later chapter.

Do not use human toothpaste for your puppy or dog. You may use baking soda or a canine toothpaste available from pet stores, with a child's soft toothbrush. Toys are available to be filled with the toothpaste so your pet can clean her teeth while chewing on them. This is a good option for an adult dog not amenable to tooth brushing. Canine toothpastes are non-foaming and are beef or peanut butter flavored. Put some paste on the toothbrush or wet the brush and dip it in baking soda. Ask your dog to "stand," pull back her lips on her upper or lower teeth and gently brush them, being careful not to scratch her gums or lips. Do a few strokes then let her lick the paste off; it's made for licking. Repeat until the job is done or the puppy gets restless. If she objects to the brushing do only a little of it for the first time. Try it once a week until it becomes routine to her, then clean your puppy's teeth about once a month.

If you have gotten your puppy used to having her mouth touched and handled, she probably won't object to tooth brushing. When I tried this on Kali she surprised me by staying still for it. Copper was curious and asked for it, too, and let me do it. As your dog gets older, you may need to have her teeth professionally cleaned every few years by a veterinarian under light anesthetic. This is simple and safe and not terribly expensive. The main reason for brushing a puppy's clean new baby teeth is to get her used to the handling. If she is four to six months old, you may see a tooth falling out with the brushing. Puppies change their baby teeth for an adult set at this age, which is why they need to chew on everything.

Administering Oral Medications

There will be times when you need to give your puppy or dog a pill, a homeopathic remedy, or a liquid medication. If she has been taught to "stand" and accept handling the process is quick and easy. If she has not, you may have a battle on your hands. To give a dog a pill, grasp the top of her muzzle with your thumb and index finger on the upper lips. She will open her mouth. Press her upper lips in to cover her teeth and she cannot close her mouth or bite you. Take the pill in your other hand and place it as far back as you can reach, past her tongue and into her throat. Release her lips, holding her muzzle shut, and stroke her throat. When you see her tongue lick her lips she has swallowed. If she refuses to swallow, blow lightly into her nostrils and she will do so reflexively. If your dog is large, you may have to sit or stand behind her, clasping her seated body between your knees while using your hands to administer the pill. Make sure she doesn't cough it up again before you send her on her way.

To give a homeopathic remedy in pellet form, you may open her mouth as above and shake the pellets onto her tongue. Let her swallow them or let them melt there. Avoid touching the pellets; they are shaken into the container cap first and dropped from the cap into the dog's mouth. For small puppies, you may crush the pellets between two kitchen spoons and place the powder onto her tongue. After crushing the pellets in the spoon, you can also wet them with a few drops of distilled water. Spoon the water, or draw it into an eyedropper, to drip the mixture into the dog's mouth. For liquid homeopathic remedies, which come with eyedroppers, open the dog's mouth and drip a few drops in. You can also gently pull out the pocket of her lower lip on one side of her muzzle and put the remedy into the resulting pouch. Homeopathic remedies are prepared on sugar pellets and, once familiar with them, most dogs take them readily. They are some of Kali's favorite treats. After administering one, lift the water bowl for fifteen minutes and do not feed for half an hour.

To give a liquid medication or herb tincture, do it in the same way as the liquid homeopathic remedy. Place the drops into the lower muzzle lip pouch on the side. Do not squirt a remedy down a dog's throat as she may choke on it. You can put a few drops at a time on her tongue and let her swallow it. The taste of herbal tinctures is usually not attractive and placing them in food may be the only way to give them. Some dogs will accept pills crushed in food also, but avoid giving homeopathic remedies in this way unless your vet directs you to. Capsules may also be opened into food. For adult tough customers, bury the pill or herbal tincture in a piece of cheese or meat. My dogs will take anything that is offered in a teaspoonful of cottage cheese.

Training your puppy to accept handling young is one of the best gifts you can give her. Grooming, bathing, trips to the vet, handling, and medicating are no longer an ordeal. They are routine things to accept without stress for both the dog and the people who must work with her. They also teach your puppy to accept training and are much like nursery school would be for a human child. The dog that can be easily handled is a joy to live with and can be kept clean and healthy, and therefore happier than one who cannot.

We move from nursery school to puppy kindergarten next, with some basic learning about living in the human family-pack.

basic puppy training

Experts believe that a dog's temperament and personality are set and established by the time she is four months old. The first eight weeks of life are for socialization in the litter with puppies and other dogs. The raised-alone bottled-fed puppy never reacts normally to other canines and if a female who was raised this way is bred she will likely not be an adequate mother. From eight weeks to four months is the time for socialization with people. This is the period when the techniques of the last two chapters are necessary for the dog to develop normally and be well-adjusted in the family-pack. A puppy that is not socialized to people at this time will never bond fully with a guardian or make a good pet. Most people bring their puppies home at seven or eight weeks of age; until they are seven weeks old they still need their mothers and litter mates. This leaves only two short months for optimal socialization to occur.

With this in mind, you cannot wait until admission to obedience class at six months to start your dog's education. If you do, obedience will be very hard work and your dog may never be fully trained in the skills needed to live successfully in your family. Many people teach only house-training to young puppies and nothing else until their puppy's house-training is finished. Those who teach their puppies more are much happier with their pets, and their puppies are much happier with them. The puppy that had no education, or none until six months, is too often the problem dog who is shifted from one home to another and who may die unwanted in a shelter. This is a shame, as early puppy training is simple and fun for both people and dogs. Early training is based on play and games that bond the dog and person into a loving team.

Early puppy training, and all rational dog training, is done a few minutes a day every day and is based on praise and "no." When a dog does something you want to reinforce, praise her for it immediately and every time so she will repeat the action to earn your approval. Praise is verbal; say "good girl" or "good puppy" in a light, bright voice. Low volume is enough, just sound happy. Use her name. Food rewards should be only an occasional thing; if you need her to come and have no treat in your hand, will she still respond? I like to save food rewards for the end of a training session and then use a small bite of something she really likes. Too many biscuits make a dog fat and you don't need that, either.

A mailing and packaging store near where I live has a canine resident named Goldie, a Doberman-mix. On the wall beside the counter hangs a string with a bell on the end and a box containing dog biscuits. When people come into the store, Goldie hits the bell with her paw or nose and waits for her biscuit. A sign over the box says, "One is fine, three is too many." It's the same in puppy training, give a tidbit once at the end of the session, but it's best not to tempt your pet to perform by using food. She will perform willingly and gladly for your praise, as long as you are consistent in giving it.

Proper Discipline and Getting Through the Terrible Chews

On the other side of the training scale is "no." This is spoken in a deep, growling, drawn-out voice that sounds like a mother dog's discipline to her litter. It is not a yell or a shout. With a very young puppy, use the "no," and if she persists reinforce it by picking her up and distracting her. If she is chewing on your shoes (which shouldn't be in reach anyhow), say "no," take the shoe away, and give her something legal to chew on. On your pup's truly bratty days, when she insists on going back to the misdeed again and again, put her in her crate for a ten-minute time out. Ignore her totally there. For an older puppy, you can ignore her for half an hour.

Disciplining a puppy does not mean hitting her. Never strike a dog with your hand, with a newspaper, or with anything else. Doing so will not make her behave. It will only make her hand-shy, eventually defiant, and possibly a biter later. If you have chosen a puppy that is number three or four on the puppy aptitude scale, you have a pet that will look to you and do her best to please you. Harsh training will not be necessary, and doing it will only ruin a loving temperament. A puppy is very much like a human infant. You want to teach her, not scare her or beat her into submission. Consistent praise for things you wish to reinforce and a consistent "no" for things you disapprove of, are all you need.

It also makes sense to puppy-proof your house. If you leave shoes on the floor, they will be chewed on, so don't leave them in reach. A child's classic excuse for not handing in homework is "the puppy ate it." While a puppy is teething she will chew on anything and, as with a human baby, everything is investigated by putting it in her mouth. You can't stop her from chewing—her gums itch and hurt—but you can provide safe things for her to chew on and keep unsafe things away from her. If you find her chewing something forbidden, say "no" and take the object away. Give her instead a rawhide bone or a toy and praise her when she takes it. When teething ends, most of the need to chew on illegal things ends with it. If you have been consistent, by that time she will know which are her toys (that she may chew) and which are your toys (that she may not). In the meantime, whenever your puppy is loose in your house, you must keep an eye on her and keep things that she could damage or could hurt her out of reach.

Along with everything else during teething, your puppy will most likely try to chew on you. This is not to be allowed. If she bites at your fingers, say "no" and close your hand or move it away from her. Anytime she bites, say "no" and stop playing with her for a few minutes. If she continues after that, give her time out in her crate. If she still persists, hold her muzzle closed gently with your fingers and say "no" again. She will not like this and after a couple of times will not risk it happening to her. A puppy should never think it is acceptable to chew on any human. She is tiny and cute now but will grow quickly, and her teeth will also, and the habit is a problem in a grown dog. Nor may she chew on her collar or leash. Disengage her teeth from the object and say "no." If she persists, clamp her mouth shut again for a moment. Be gentle but consistent and firm. Persistent collar and leash chewing can also be stopped by rubbing the portion she chews on with hot sauce or cayenne pepper mixed with water. Once will be enough.

Leash Training

Your puppy is already used to wearing a collar and now it's time to try the leash. You may already be using a finger through her collar to hold her back at times and this is a good preliminary leash exercise. If you have not done so before, try the following. Put a finger through the puppy's collar and tell her to "wait." At the same time, put your other hand on her chest to hold her still and keep her from pulling or twisting. Do not scold her for the struggle, just ignore it. When she becomes still praise her and let her go. Do this a few times a day, so she learns that a pull on her collar means she must hold still and wait until you release her. This can be done with even an eight-week-old puppy.[1]

When using a command that does not invite action, as in "stand," "wait," or "no," do not use the puppy's name with it. Save the name for when you praise her and when you wish her to actually move or do something. Once she knows her name, saying it will start her moving toward you. Use that tendency and reinforce it by saying her name when you wish her to move. To use her name and then tell her *not* to move, contradicts her instincts and confuses her. While she is learning her name, use it while talking to her as often as possible.

Once she knows "wait," the next step is the leash. Attach it to her collar and let her walk around dragging it. Let her sniff and paw at it but not chew it. Play with her while the leash is attached, and feed her with it still on, but do not pick it up yet. After a few days and play sessions dragging the leash, pick it up but hold still. If she has learned the lesson of "wait," the pull on her collar will make

1 Gwen Bailey, *The Perfect Puppy*, p. 50.

her hold still and wait for you. Praise her and let the leash drop again. Give this a few tries, and when she has learned to wait at the tug of the leash, take the next step.

Pick up the leash, call the puppy's name and invite her to "come on." Pat your left leg and squeak that special palm size squeaky toy you bought when you brought her home. With the toy as lure, bring your puppy to your left side and take a few steps, urging her along. She will move beside you, sometimes only raggedly, and sometimes only to try to get the toy. Hold the toy on your left side close to your body and praise her for following. Try this a couple of times a day for about five minutes. Do it indoors at first and use the squeaky toy. You may occasionally use a food treat or try this off leash (safely indoors or in the yard). Pick training times when she is too tired to resist you and stop before she loses interest. Keep the training separate from elimination walks or do not start the training session until she has eliminated. End each session with a few minutes' play with the toy or give her the treat you have used to lure her.

Using the toy, your voice, and her curiosity, try to get the puppy to walk with you if only a few steps at first. Keep the leash loose and if she starts to pull, stop walking and stand still. The puppy will keep going for another step or two and then the leash will stop her. At the same time that she feels the quick tug on her collar, say "no." When she stops pulling, lure her with the toy to bring her back to your side, praise her, say her name and "come on," and start again. When you wish to change directions, use the command and the squeaky toy to get her attention. She must learn to watch where you are going and go with you.[2]

Never allow your puppy to pull. She must know very early that pulling ends the walk and is uncomfortable even in the flat collar she is wearing. Hold the leash short enough so that the dog is kept to your left side, and when starting or bringing her back, start her from your left again. This is a preliminary to the obedience "heel" command. For now, be patient and do the exercise for five minutes twice a day. Start indoors, then move outside in your yard. When she has the hang of it, try a real walk where there are few distractions, keeping it short the first few times. The puppy will eventually learn to walk with you. Take each step

2 Ibid., p. 154-157.

of the process slowly and don't rush. If she continues to pull, work more often on holding her by the collar and the command to "wait."

Stop immediately when the puppy pulls ahead. To let her do it now will encourage her to drag you on the leash continually. This will start a habit more difficult to break later in a dog that is growing larger and stronger every day. Keeping her from pulling from the start makes her a joy to walk with once she learns how to do it with you. If your breed is one that is bred for hauling and pulling, like Siberian Huskies, this exercise may take much more time and patience than with other dogs. Start it young and make the effort; by the time your dog is grown she will have learned to walk quietly with you on leash.

Once your puppy can walk reasonably on her leash try a bonding exercise. Clip the six-foot leash to the puppy's collar and loop the other end around your left wrist. Now go about your day while the puppy must follow along. You can be reading, walking, doing housework, talking on the phone; the puppy is tied to you and must follow everywhere you move. Notice her sometimes but mostly go about your work. Do this for an hour a couple of times a week. It's a great way to keep an eye on the puppy during house-training and it teaches her both to watch you and cooperate with your movements. The puppy that watches you for her behavior cues is very easy to train. You can also do this with a new adult dog who has not yet learned to look to you or obey you.

Teaching Your Puppy to Sit, Lie Down, and Come

It is very easy to teach your puppy to sit. Hold her food bowl, a treat, or a toy about two feet over her head, then move the object and your hand back. In order to see what you are holding, the puppy's head also goes back and she will automatically sit. Use the command "sit" as she does so and praise her. Do this once, then give her what you have tempted her with. Do the exercise before you feed her each time, before you give her a rawhide bone or toy, and before you let her outside in your yard or when you are going out with her on leash. Use the command consistently, praise her immediately when she sits, then give her the reward—the food or toy or the open door. She will learn the "sit" quickly and easily this way.

To teach her to lie down first have her sit. Then using the squeaky toy or a bit of food, and putting your hand in front of her nose, lure her to the ground. When her head goes down the rest of her will follow. As soon as her body goes down, praise her and give her the toy or a pat. The command is "down." Some dogs respond to hand signals for this sooner than to the voice. If I tap the floor with my finger, Kali goes down, and strangely it's her most reliable command.

"Down" is an entirely different command than "off." "Down" means the dog must take the lying down position. "Off " means to get off of something she is not permitted to be on. ("Off " as in "get off the couch.") It is also used when a puppy jumps up on you or on anyone else. The command is usually preceded by "no," as in "no, off." When she does as she is told, praise her but only when all four feet are on the floor. "Off " is something learned by experience, not taught as a training exercise.

If your puppy jumps on you it's a habit you will want to stop early, using the "off" command. As soon as she puts her feet on you, take her two front paws and hold them up higher than is comfortable for her. Say "no, off" without her name, and continue holding her paws. When she becomes worried about not getting them back again, let her go. Do this every time and the bad habit will not take hold. Everyone the puppy jumps on must use the procedure if it is to work. Otherwise, she will decide who she can and can't jump up on and act according-ly.[3] My dogs, for example, never jump up on me but they do on other people because few are willing to stop them. This exercise can be done with adult dogs as well as puppies. It is not safe to knee a dog to make her "off." The movement could injure her heart, which is positioned close to the chest surface.

Begin teaching your puppy to come by calling her to do so every time you feed her. Say "Kali, come" in an excited voice, and praise her when she comes. Have her "sit," then give her the bowl of food. At other times, bring out a biscuit or a squeaky toy, show it to her or squeak it and call her to come. Praise her and give her the biscuit or the toy to play with for a few minutes. Use food rewards more frequently for this than for other exercises. Start teaching the "come" indoors and do not move outside with it until your puppy comes every time you

3 Monks of New Skete, *The Art of Raising a Puppy*, p. 209.

holistic puppy

call. Outdoors, only practice it in a fenced yard. Use toys or an occasional tidbit—coming must be very desirable. Kneel down on the ground with arms opened wide, call her name and "come." Praise her lavishly for obeying.

Do this exercise at every opportunity many times a day. Always have some kind of reward. Only do it, however, when you think she will respond, usually when she would be coming to you anyhow. Do not call her when she is distracted with something else—go to her if you want her. Rack up as many successes as you can with this one and as often as you can. You may do the same exercise with grown dogs. If you ever want your puppy or dog to come reliably, you must absolutely *never* call her to you for punishment or to do anything with her she may not like. If you need to discipline her, cut toenails, bathe her, or give her a pill, go and get her. One mistake with this and it's all over. Call her to you just once to punish her or for something she won't like and she will never come reliably again. In obedience classes the "come" is the last thing taught, because it's the most crucial. Make it a puppy game, but call her only when you think she will obey, and always use some form of tempting reward.

Follow every training session with playtime, and playtime with a trip outside to eliminate and then a meal. When training and obeying signals that food or a game will follow, it is always welcomed. Make training sessions fun and end them quickly if your puppy gets tired or begins to lose interest. A small puppy has a very short attention span. Keep training sessions to five minutes at first and extend them to ten minutes as she grows older. Do not exceed ten minutes for a puppy under six months of age and do not exceed fifteen or twenty minutes for a grown dog. Sessions can be frequent if they are kept short. Emphasize the praise and reinforce successes rather than the mistakes and the "no."

To encourage your puppy to watch you, tap your face beside your eye and say "watch me" or "look" in a bright voice. A hard stare can be as much discipline as a strong verbal "no" and a loving look as much praise as any treat to a puppy who will look you in the eye. Encourage this but don't force it. Eye contact means dominance and the puppy learns that *you* are dominant. Long loving communing with the eyes usually happens in a trained adult dog who has learned to love and trust you.

How to Discourage Begging for Food and Attention

You must teach your dog not to beg for human food. When you are eating your puppy stays in her crate. Animal behaviorists say that your dog or puppy should not eat until after you finish or, if you feed her first, take a bite of something yourself before giving her the meal. You may also feed her at times away from your own mealtimes. The message here is that your food is your own and has nothing to do with the dog. Do not talk to her while you are eating and ignore all begging for food at any time. If you wish to give your dog table scraps, and they are nutritional ones, wait until after your meal is finished. Scrape your plate into the puppy's own bowl, open the crate, make her "sit," then allow her to eat.

Be tough about this with puppies. Once your dog is grown and not a nuisance, you may let her out of her crate while you eat. Ignore all begging and don't give her anything from the table. Pleading eyes are hard to resist but a dog that begs or takes food off your plate or table is a pest. A little hardness of heart now makes a difference for the rest of the dog's life. If your dog snatches food off a table or counter, crate her or put her outside while you are cooking, as well.

Copper is an inveterate beggar and can get pushy. Kali seems to have been trained on this score, as she lies quietly beside the table at mealtimes and doesn't ask for food. However, she bolts hers down faster than any dog I've ever seen and then tries to take Copper's. Dusty could make anything fall off of a plate, table, stove, or counter and always looked totally innocent as she caught it falling. She could also manifest whatever food she wanted, usually pizza or chocolate. The antics will seem funny until the first time the dog grabs your dinner, or the first time you have guests, and then it's not funny at all. The older dog you adopt may not have been table trained and may have to spend dinner time crated or outside.

For an adult dog who is an impossible food moocher enlist the aid of a friend. This is an exercise you must not do yourself. Ask the friend to come and eat with you, and expect your dog to show her worst table manners. She may push and paw at the visitor, try to grab food, nose her plate, whine, and otherwise be a nuisance. Your guest will be provided with a bowl containing a few teaspoonsful of cayenne pepper or hot sauce. At the height of your dog's bad act, ask the guest to "give her some." The guest has been coached to do so but to dip it in the pepper first. She feeds the dog, who will run for her water bowl but be otherwise unharmed, and the dog will never beg from her again. You may try this with a variety of dinner friends until the dog stops begging permanently. An animal's guardian is never to do this; your dog must take food from you every day and may not distinguish table food from her own proper food bowl. It is a risk—she may refuse to accept food from you. The method works for a grown dog who is a nuisance at mealtimes.

Your puppy must also learn to stay quietly in her crate when you put her there, even if you leave the house. She may have a toy or rawhide bone inside with her to keep her busy. Your first reaction to a small puppy's whining in the crate—assuming that she is dry, fed, and doesn't need to eliminate—is to totally ignore it. Any response from you will seem a reinforcement, as she is whining to get your attention. If you can totally ignore her, she will soon stop since she is not getting the response she wants. Take her out of the crate when *you* are ready and not before, and take her out only when she is quiet.

As she gets older and more used to the crate as her home inside a home the whining usually stops. If it does not, you may have to take other measures. Start by a harsh "no," which can be emphasized by tapping loudly on the top of the box. Ignore her again after that. When she stops fussing, praise her and let her out. At night try covering the mesh door of the crate (or all of it if the crate is a wire one) with a towel. If she can no longer see what's going on outside the crate, and if it's dark and quiet, she may give up and go to sleep.

When you place the puppy in her crate to go out make sure she has a toy to chew on, preferably one she hasn't seen in a few days to make it more desirable. You can rotate a few toys to keep them interesting. Avoid making a fuss about either leaving or coming home. Be matter of fact about it and say no goodbyes. If you take leaving calmly your puppy will, too. It's not a big deal. If you think she may be crying while you're away test her out. Put her in the crate, pick up your keys and backpack, and leave. Stay in hearing distance, however, perhaps on the porch, and listen quietly. If you hear whining that doesn't stop soon, bound back in and say a sharp "no," then leave again. Listen for her crying and repeat the "no" if you need to. If you are leaving to go to work you may enlist a neighbor to help with this. Once your puppy thinks that you are always listening and will always discipline her the crying will stop.

No matter how much your puppy cries, never let an untrained, unreliable dog loose in your house while you go away. This is an open invitation to come home and find your linoleum ripped, your couch chewed up, and feathers from your bed pillows all over the house. Some dogs suffer from separation anxiety. In a dog pack the pack goes everywhere together. You are your dog or puppy's pack, so why are you leaving her there by herself? The crate is the one humane answer to preventing such destruction and has saved the lives of many dogs that would have otherwise lost their homes through such behavior. Your dog will outgrow her chewing and destructive phases but it may take until she is two years old or more. In the meantime, the crate is your best ally and hers. By the time she no longer needs it your dog will not want to be without it. It will be her home, den, and resting place. Leave it in the kitchen for her to come and go into as she wishes.

This is only a beginning of early puppy training. Please understand that though I have raised many puppies I am not a dog trainer nor an obedience expert. For real training or problem solving with your dog, seek the advice of an experienced, humane trainer or behaviorist. I recommend Kindergarten Puppy Training for all puppies and obedience classes for your adopted adult whether purebred or mixed-bred. The classes will solve many problems and, better yet, prevent them.

optimal puppy nutrition

People come to me with all kinds of dog problems, usually health problems that no standard allopathic vet can acceptably solve. I always have the same three questions for them: What are you feeding? Have you antidoted the vaccination side-effects? And are you using a holistic veterinarian? Food is the first and foremost way to solve most pet problems. The other two questions are discussed in the next chapter. The old adage "you are what you eat" is as applicable to pets as to people. People learning to be aware of their own diets and what they feed their children are also learning to apply this knowledge to feeding their pets. To have a healthy dog or puppy this is the place to start.

Human old age is plagued with a variety of ills. Heart dis-ease or cancer kill about two thirds of all people in the West. These dis-eases were barely known a hundred years ago. People's life expectancy is not increasing. It is probably decreasing, and our quality of life is certainly declining. Dogs are experiencing the same decline and the same dis-eases. Cancer and heart dis-ease were unknown in dogs fifty years ago. The life expectancy of working sheep dogs thirty or forty years ago was about twenty-five years. Today most dogs are old by ten and almost all are dead by fifteen. The blame for this decline may be placed on the poor quality of the food we feed ourselves and our animals, along with the chemicalization of food and medical treatment. Our planet's increasing levels of air, water, and soil pollution, soil and mineral depletion, contamination with toxic chemicals, preservatives and pesticides, growth stimulant hormones in plants and meat sources, and invasive and poisonous medical treatments are shortening all our lives.

Don't Be Misled by Commercial Advertising

If our dogs are to live long, healthy lives free of chronic dis-eases, cancer, and heart failure, proper feeding from the start is essential. The bag at the supermarket that says "all you add is love" is not telling you the whole story, nor is the food claiming it's a "premium blend," "nutritionally complete," or "everything your dog or puppy needs." You will never find a nutritionally complete pet food in the supermarket and even if you buy an optimal holistic pet food you will need more than this. The pet food industry has spent many millions of dollars in advertising to tell you not to feed your dog human food or table scraps. This is another fable, as the best diet you can feed your dog is a *carefully designed* program of home-cooking that is natural and organic.

An amazing variety of pet ills disappear within weeks after changing the dog to a holistic diet. The foremost of these is skin problems, even down to dogs covered head to foot with sores and having hair loss so extensive that they are actually bald. All coat problems respond to an optimal diet, including oiliness, hair loss, rashes and sores, body odor, excessive scratching, and shedding. Fleas are less likely to attack a dog that is well fed, or to cause skin allergies if they do. Flea infestations on a naturally fed dog are easily dealt with. Chronic gas, diarrhea, and digestive disturbances heal quickly on natural, preservative-free foods. Hyperactivity, short attention span, some aggressiveness, and many behavior problems also disappear and even seizures can be reduced or eliminated without medication on the proper diet.

The lethargic dog that lies around all day can come alive with good feeding. Liver failure and kidney dis-ease does not develop in older pets that have been properly fed and pets already manifesting these dis-eases are considerably helped. Autoimmune and glandular dis-eases, diabetes, hyper- or hypothyroid and heart dis-ease need not manifest. On a proper diet cancer is less likely to end your dog's life. Arthritis and hip dysplasia are vitamin deficiency dis-eases that can be prevented in puppies and minimized in older dogs.

Why are our pets missing out when packaged pet foods are supposed to be everything our animals need? Commercial pet food companies spend much more of their many millions of dollars on advertising than they do on what goes into the bag or can. They are in the business to make money, not to help animals. To do so, industry competition decrees that they spend as little as possible on ingredients and production costs and sell for as high a price and as high a profit as they can get. Advertising to gain the attention of consumers is endemic and those who buy the product pay for it. Prices must also be kept competitive, as the consumer is likely to choose the product with the lowest price from a variety of brands that all claim to have everything your dog needs. With advertising costs figured in, not much of the money is left to pay for the food itself.

Supermarket pet food companies use the cheapest ingredients they can get. Meat by-products and offal comprise forty percent of dog food and the other sixty percent is comprised of grain and soy meal. The terms "meat by-products" and "offal" mean slaughterhouse wastes like cow hooves and horns, bones, organs not used for human consumption, cow udders, lungs, pig snouts, tails, intestines, skin and hair, glands, chicken feathers and beaks, feet and claws. Anything not acceptable for human consumption may be (and is) used in pet foods, including dis-eased organs and animal parts, tumors and cancerous tissues, and spoiled, rancid, and moldy flesh. Bloody sawdust from packing plant floors can be included in pet foods—blood is called a "by-product" and sawdust "vegetable fiber". Dis-eased and dying animals and those that die on the feed lots—often from the overwhelming hormones and chemicals that are fed them on their way to market—are used in pet food. This comprises forty percent of the food. The grain and "vegetable fiber" that makes up the other sixty percent is made of grains unacceptable for human use, usually because of rancidity and contamination including bacterial contamination. Ground-up corn husks and peanut shells come under the category of "vegetable fiber."

Meat source animals today are raised on fodder laden with pesticides, antibiotics, and hormones. Many are factory-farmed under horrific crowding and extreme stress conditions. The toxins become part of the meat and tissues, especially the eliminative organs, bones, and fat that are included in pet food. The chemicals do not leave the animals' bodies before slaughter and are known to be implicated in the raising rates of cancer and birth defects. Illegal residues of chemical contamination reach human food meat departments every day. No one is counting where pet foods are concerned. Pet food plants are not even inspected. The ingredients are steamed to kill bacteria (heat also kills desirable vitamins and enzymes), but chemical residues are not heat-affected.

Pet food companies take these slaughterhouse wastes and garbage and add a variety of chemicals to them. Artificial colors and flavorings are added to make the mix look like meat again and to make it more appealing both to dogs and to human buyers. These chemicals have been linked to epilepsy, cancer, birth defects, autism, hyperactivity, nervousness and anxiety, hostility, and behavior problems. They may increase dogs' sensitivity to fatal viruses. Chemical preservatives are added to keep the fat from going rancid. These have been implicated in liver and kidney dis-ease, behavior problems, slow growth, metabolic disorders, increased cholesterol, allergic reactions, baldness, cancer, and brain defects. Natural preservatives are readily available that cause none of these ills. Many canned and semi-moist pet foods contain lethal amounts of lead, salt, and sugar. These cause damaged nervous, immune, enzyme, and red blood cell systems, heart dis-ease and high blood pressure, vomiting and mineral depletion, hypoglycemia, diabetes, skin and hair problems, diarrhea, and obesity.

Three chemicals are most prevalent in dog and puppy foods—BHA, BHT, and Ethoxyquin. All three preservatives are implicated in a lot of pet dis-eases, from skin problems to liver and kidney failures, from allergies to cancer, from birth defects to immune-related dis-eases of all types. These are prevalent in virtually all supermarket dog and puppy foods, along with the chemicals and horrors listed above. While preservatives to prevent rancidity are necessary, toxic chemicals are not. Vitamins C, E, and A—all healthy and needed in animal and human diets—are superior and proven substitutes. Likewise, colorings and flavorings are not needed, or natural ones can be provided, when reasonable quality ingredients are used. This is not an impossible dream but is available almost anywhere in a new line of noncommercial dog foods.

The Safest and Healthiest Food Choices

These are the *preservative-free* foods that are so essential to healthy feeding for your dog. Preservative free does not mean that there are no preservatives or additives but that the preservatives and additives are natural and non-chemical and that they add to the food's nutrition rather than cause dis-ease. Their manufacturers are usually small companies, which do not waste their money or yours with hard-sell advertising. They base their products on high quality or even organic sources of protein, grain, and vegetables. By providing these foods for your pet, or better yet cooking for them at home (see below), a myriad of dis-eases may be prevented or cured. Your dog will live longer, live healthier, be better behaved, more beautiful, and will certainly live a happier life.

The difference has to be seen to be believed. Many people do nothing more than change their dog's food and within a few weeks are totally amazed. Better yet, start your puppy on these clean foods to begin with and prevent all the diseases from the start. Nonchemicalized foods will increase your dog's lifespan and quality of life and they cost little more than supermarket brands. Should you want to go all the way and learn the simple things your puppy needs for health, you may also choose to prepare the meat, grains, and vegetables at home. If you cook natural foods for your family, what you feed your children can be the basis of what you feed your pet. A well-made, home-cooked diet is the best that you can do for your dog. However, if you are not able to cook organic and natural-only, if you cannot observe the nutritional requirement needs, or if you simply do not wish to cook, a preservative-free pet food with a few supplements added will still keep your dog healthy and happy.

Preservative-free foods and dog biscuits are becoming more and more available. You will not find them in supermarkets or standard veterinarians' offices but pet shop chains, holistic veterinarians, and some dog groomers carry them. They can also be ordered by mail through holistic pet catalogs or direct from the companies. Some sources are available by mail order only. The foods are made in puppy blends and blends for adult dogs and seniors. The cost averages about a dollar per pound. Your pet will eat less of these than other foods, as the nutritional content is much higher. When shopping, look for the bag that does not list in its ingredients BHA, BHT, or Ethoxyquin and states that it is naturally preserved.

Also look for a dog food that does not include the major allergy-causing agents. In dogs these most frequent allergens are similar to what irritates humans. The top allergen for puppies and dogs is beef—the main by-product in virtually all supermarket foods. Most preservative-free optimal pet foods are made from lamb and rice, chicken and rice, or even venison or rabbit and rice as their primary ingredients. Other prime sources of pet food allergies are cow's milk, yeast and yeast-containing products, corn and corn oil, pork, turkey, eggs, fish and fish oil, and wheat.[1] Not all dogs have difficulty with these foods but many may develop allergies to them, usually over a period of years.

Other allergens may include beans, peas, nuts, shellfish, cruciferous vegetables like broccoli or cauliflower, pineapple, tomatoes, cabbage, any individual fruit, mushrooms, or any spice. Many pets are allergic to one or more of the commercial preservatives and chemicals. Chocolate or alcohol should never be fed to dogs—they can cause fatal toxicities. It is best to avoid feeding vegetables from the nightshade family—tomatoes, eggplant, peppers, and potatoes—especially if your older dog is arthritic or comes from a large breed prone to joint dis-ease.

Some of the allergic symptoms that good feeding prevents or eliminates include itchiness and scratching, every type of skin problem, gastrointestinal symptoms like finicky eating, diarrhea, vomiting, and gas, pancreatic damage, liver and kidney damage, mucus, weight gain, chronic fatigue, bowel inflammation, heart dis-ease, seizures, respiratory symptoms, hyperactivity, and

1 Alfred Plechner, DVM, *Pet Allergies: Remedies for an Epidemic*, (Inglewood, CA, Very Healthy Enterprises, 1986), p. 20.

temperament problems. It makes very good sense to feed preservative-free foods to both your dog and your family. If the food costs a little more your smaller veterinary bills will more than make up for it. No wonder the number of "miracle cures" that changing dogs' diets accomplishes.

Dogs are primarily carnivores and with one exception require high protein (meat) diets to be healthy. The ten essential amino acids dogs require are not readily available without feeding meat. They require much higher protein levels than people do but somewhat less than cats do. Cats cannot live at all on meat-free diets and dogs can be raised vegetarian only with great care. I do not recommend trying it, though I am a vegetarian myself. Dogs that suffer seizures should not be fed meat. If changing to a preservative-free diet does not stop the seizures from occurring after a trial of a few months, a vegetarian pet food or home vegetarian cooking is the next step. PetGuard offers such a prepared, preservative-free food. Vegetarian dogs require vitamin and other supplementation to their diets, available from some holistic pet catalogs, but the seizures will usually stop on this diet.

Traditional nutritional information states that grown dogs require about twenty percent protein and twenty percent fat (forty percent protein together with fat), and sixty percent carbohydrates (dry food measurement). The protein and fat mentioned include meat and meat products, poultry, eggs, cottage cheese, fish, and oils; carbohydrates are vegetables, starches, grains, or cereals. These protein values are not enough for puppies, who require about sixty percent protein together with fats. Some holistic veterinarians recommend the higher protein ratio for adult dogs as well. A few of the preservative-free dog foods are listed as optimal for both adult dogs and puppies. These contain the ideal of about sixty to sixty-three percent of protein plus fat, with about twenty-three percent carbohydrates.

I recommend the higher protein-fat levels for both adult dogs and puppies, as long as they are fed from quality ingredients. Some sources blame too-high protein levels for kidney failure in old dogs; this will not happen with quality protein ingredients. If your dog or puppy's flesh feels mushy under the skin she is getting enough protein. If she feels hard and well muscled her protein levels are correct for her needs. If your pet seems to have little hair that grows very slowly, this is another indication of more protein needed. (Most puppies don't begin developing typical coats for their breed until they are a year old.) If you decide to do home cooking, be aware of these nutritional percentages and levels. If you buy your preservative-free dog food by the bag or can, also be aware of the amounts of protein, fats, and carbohydrates in the brand.

Meat and grains are not the only things your puppy or dog needs. Vegetables are necessary, too. A small amount of grated raw carrot or any other raw vegetable (avoid tomatoes or peppers) may be added to your puppy's diet. For a puppy under six months, limit these to about a teaspoonful a day. You may add small amounts of grated fruit as well but only small amounts as they may cause diarrhea in pets unused to them. You may also supplement your pet's preservative-free dog food diet with a spoonful of yogurt, cottage cheese, other mild cheese, soft cooked egg, or raw meat (not pork—its chemical levels are too high and it may contain trichinosis). It is fine to give your pet table scraps but only if they are healthy, natural, and preservative free. Avoid allergen suspects or give them only occasionally, and avoid hot spices of any kind. Dogs have likes and dislikes and you will become aware of what your puppy's food tastes are. Copper's favorite food is cottage cheese, while Kali loves yogurt, and both dogs are popcorn and pizza hounds.

Supplementing Your Dog's Diet

Whether you are feeding preservative-free, packaged dog food or cooking at home, I recommend giving your puppy or adult dog a daily pet vitamin, a balanced pet or health food store mineral mix and some vitamin C. Powdered sodium ascorbate C tastes delightful to dogs and people and a little bit goes a very long way. Add a 400 IU vitamin E capsule a couple of times a week after six months of age, and half to one teaspoonful of olive or flax seed oil a couple of times a week. These are fed by mixing them with food.

If your puppy is a large breed, veterinarian Larry Bernstein also recommends supplementing with glucosamine and chondroitin (Cosequin) as a preventive for hip and joint problems. Dosage is by body weight, using 500 mg two or three times a day for an adult German shepherd and less for smaller dogs and puppies. Glucosamine and chondroitin are available together from health food stores. In large-breed puppies vitamin C is essential. If your puppy or dog has skin problems add half to one teaspoonful of kelp powder, blue green algae, or Barley Dog, or about 10 mg of zinc daily to her food. Different practitioners and holistic veterinarians recommend different supplementation protocols and there are many positive books, recipes, and ideas on the subject. Remember, too, that each dog and puppy is an individual with her own needs.

Vitamin C is one of the miracle foods for both pets and people. Veterinarian Wendell Belfield discovered that hip and joint dis-ease in dogs is a form of scurvy, the vitamin C deficiency dis-ease. The spinal myelopathy that kills so many Doberman pinschers and other large-breed dogs may also be a C deficiency. He experimented with breeding hip dysplastic German shepherds and feeding the pregnant dams and resulting puppies vitamin C. These puppies would have been expected to develop hip dysplasia but did not. He also discovered that feeding vitamin C can minimize hip damage in young dogs already manifesting the dis-ease. Arthritic dogs benefit from vitamin C, as do arthritic people, and minerals are also important.

This is Dr. Belfield's daily vitamin protocol for weaned puppies:

Multiple vitamin and mineral tablet, follow directions on the bottle. Begin vitamin E at six months old.

For vitamin C use the following:

First six months: *small breeds* 250 mg; *medium breeds* 500 mg.

Six months to a year, gradually increasing to adult levels: *small breeds* 250-500 mg; *medium breeds* 500-1500 mg.

First four months: *large breeds* gradually increase from 500 to 1000 mg; *giant breeds* 750-2000 mg.

Four to eighteen months gradually increasing to adult levels: *large breeds* 1000-3000 mg; *giant breeds* 2000 to 6000 mg. (1000 mg = 1 gram).

For adult dogs:
Multiple vitamin and mineral tablet, follow directions on the bottle.
Vitamin C and E:

	Small	Medium	Large	Giant
Vitamin C	500-1500 mg	1500-3000	3000-6000	6000-7500
Vitamin E	100 IU	200 IU	200 IU	400 IU

For pregnant and lactating dogs, and dogs under high stress:
Use the higher values for vitamin C and increase vitamin E to 400 IU for *large breeds* and to 600 IU for *giant breeds*.

For aged dogs:
Multiple vitamin and mineral supplement, and vitamins C and E:

	Small	Medium	Large	Giant
Vitamin C	250-750 mg	750-1500	1500-3000	3000-4000
Vitamin E	200 IU	400 IU	400 IU	800 IU[2]

As powdered vitamin C measures 5000 mg per teaspoonful, you are actually using very little. The amounts Dr. Belfield uses are mega-doses and are high, but they are completely nontoxic. These supplements are used by mixing them with the pet's food; tablets are crushed and vitamin E capsules are punctured and squeezed onto the meal. The supplements are all normally available from health food stores, and pet-specific daily vitamins and minerals may be found at pet shops or holistic suppliers. When starting vitamin C for the first time begin with very small doses and increase gradually to prevent initial diarrhea. If despite gradual increases you reach a level where diarrhea occurs, slightly decrease the amount of C. This is your dog or puppy's bowel tolerance level for now. She may accept more or less vitamin C later. The point of bowel tolerance varies with the individual and will fluctuate with health, growth, and stress factors. The supplements should be used whether you are feeding a store-bought, preservative-free or home-cooked diet.

2 Wendell O. Belfield, DVM and Martin Zucker, *How to Have a Healthier Dog: The Benefits of Vitamins and Minerals for your Dog's Life Cycles.* (New York, NY, New American Library, 1981), p. 156-160.

If you wish to cook for your puppy or dog at home, there is a variety of holistic pet cookbooks on the market. Two good ones are Joan Harper's *The Healthy Cat and Dog Cookbook* and Juliette de Bairacli Levy's *The Complete Herbal Handbook for the Dog and Cat*. By using the correct percentages of meat protein, carbohydrates/grains, and vegetables, and adding the supplements you will have the optimal best nutrition for your pet. A preservative-free dog food with supplements is a highly respectable second choice. Supermarket foods are not to be considered. Dogs raised on a quality natural diet live free of most or all diseases. Their coats are beautiful, skins clear, and eyes bright. Their intelligence and personalities reflect their overall health and well-being. These are the dogs that have the best chance for a longer life span and problem-free old age. As guardians to these animals that give us so much, we can do no less for them.

the holistic veterinarian

Holistic or natural medicine is a new/old way of treating pets and people. Where allopathy (standard medicine) focuses on dis-ease and the suppression of symptoms by chemical drugs and surgeries, holistic medicine focuses on wellness. Every attempt is made to give animals the best options for good health daily through nutrition and supplementation and through protection against the ravages of unnecessary toxins. When dis-ease occurs the focus is on marshaling the body's natural forces to rebalance and regain the normally healthy state. In holistic medicine, symptoms are not suppressed but are treated by locating and removing their sources. Natural medicine goes back to old ways, to non-chemical answers to dis-ease, methods that support wellness and never offer harm when used appropriately. Where allopathic medicines are a trade-off of symptoms for side-effects or a suppression of one dis-ease to manifest another, holistic medicine has little or no side-effects, uncovers suppressions, and removes dis-ease completely at the source.

The Drawbacks of Allopathic Methods

In the past twenty years allopathic veterinary medicine has become increasingly chemical dependent, overly technologized, over-priced, and removed from the realities of quality of life. The human medical system did this first and medicine for animals has now followed. A woman took her dog to an off-hours veterinary emergency clinic after she thought the dog had been poisoned. Instead of treating her pet, the clinic first quoted her a list of procedures and prices and asked if she had the money for them. The list went on and on. They asked her if she could pay, by what method, asked her for payment in advance, and asked her what her price limit for healing her dog would be. The woman was appalled and kept telling them, "I don't care what it costs, just help my dog." The dog somehow survived.

I have witnessed many instances of animals subjected to allopathic drugs and chemicals, chemotherapies and surgeries, to the point where the dog spent her days lying around ill, in pain and unhappy. There is always another drug to try until the animal that may have been terminal to begin with finally dies a prolonged and miserable death, or until her person runs out of funds. I have also seen many instances of animals written off as terminal by the allopathic system who recovered easily, readily, painlessly, and completely by holistic methods that an allopathic vet either does not know about or scorns. Having watched this suffering for many years for both people and dogs, I have long decided that allopathy is unacceptable for either.

The Benefits of Holistic Treatment

Holistic veterinary treatment differs considerably from allopathic methods. It includes herbs, homeopathy, acupuncture, chiropractic, and flower essences. Natural means "from nature," not from a pharmaceutical cartel. When treatment is done in natural ways, health and vitality are supported, dis-ease is released, the damage from allopathic medications is released and removed, and the dog or puppy regains her well-being. While holistic veterinary care is not less expensive than allopathic care, its attitude is life affirming rather than money grabbing. If your vet acts otherwise, seek a new one.

When people ask me for help with their pets my first question is "What are you feeding her?" My second question is "Do you have a holistic veterinarian?" If your dog is to live a healthy long life it is absolutely essential that you find a holistic veterinarian to work with. To find such a veterinarian you may write to one of several referral organizations who will give you the phone numbers of practitioners in your area. The three foremost organizations are:

American Holistic Veterinary Medical Association
(AHVMA)
2214 Old Emmorton Rd.
Bel Air, MD 21015
Tel: (410)569-0795 FAX: (410)515-7774

Academy of Veterinary Homeopathy (AVH)
Dr. Larry Bernstein, VMD
751 NE 168th St.
N. Miami Beach, FL 33162-2427
Tel: (305)652-5372 FAX: (305)653-7244
E-mail: avh@naturalholistic.com
Web Site: www.acadvethom.org

International Veterinary Acupuncture Society (IVAS)
268 W 3rd St. Suite #4
POB 2074
Nederland, CO 80466
Tel: (303)258-3767 FAX: (303)258-0767
E-mail: IVASJAGG@msn.com

If no holistic veterinarian practices in your area, you may choose to work with one by telephone, using your allopathic vet as backup for tests the holistic practitioner may need. Some allopathic vets are willing to work this way, others are not; you will need to interview your allopathic backup to see if s/he is cooperative. In the same way you choose a practitioner for yourself, talk with your prospective holistic veterinarian before committing your pet to her care. Decide if she offers what you want for your dog or puppy and whether you feel comfortable working with her. Ask about prices and protocols. It is best to do all this while your dog or puppy is healthy, both to begin wellness care immediately and because illness or emergencies are poor times for such searches. It is best to start your puppy off with a holistic veterinarian as soon as you bring her home.

I highly recommend that you do some basic background reading on natural methods so you understand what your vet is doing. Many holistic veterinarians provide an information packet, but reading a book or two is more useful. A number of excellent books on natural pet care and healing are available. Two such books are my own *Natural Healing for Dogs and Cats* and *The Natural Remedy Book for Dogs and Cats*. Both are available from The Crossing Press. Other books are listed in the bibliography.

The Risks of Vaccination

The first and possibly most major philosophical difference you will find between allopathic and holistic methods is the routine vaccinations for puppies and dogs. By faithfully giving puppies their series of shots and continuing with annual boosters, dog guardians have been told that they are doing their best to keep their animals healthy. Evidence is growing for both pets and people, however, that this is just the opposite. Vaccinations are being increasingly implicated as the source of a great deal of harm. Not only are vaccinations proving to be ineffective, with animals quite frequently developing the dis-eases they have been vaccinated against, but they are being discovered as the source of a number of serious and chronic dis-ease states. This is as true for human children as for pets.

In the process of vaccination, antibodies to a number of dis-eases are introduced into the bloodstream of a puppy. The first standard puppy shot, given at seven or eight weeks, consists of antigens for distemper, adenovirus type 2, parainfluenza, and parvovirus (DA2PL-Parvo). This is repeated at ten or eleven weeks when a vaccination for corona virus is added. At thirteen or fourteen weeks, the puppy is given another combination repeating all of the above, plus a nasal administration of bordatella vaccine and an injection for lyme dis-ease. At sixteen or seventeen weeks, further doses of lyme, bordatella, and parvovirus antigens are given, plus a rabies shot.

When a puppy or person is exposed naturally to a dis-ease it usually enters the body by breathing the virus in. The healthy body's normal response to the exposure is to create antibodies as an immune defense for the dis-ease, one dis-ease at a time, as exposure causes the antibodies to be needed. Beginning immunities are transmitted to new puppies through their mothers' milk. When combination vaccines are given, a number of antigens (substances that promote creation of antibodies) are introduced at once in a way unnatural to the immune system's programming. Because of the method of introduction (through the bloodstream instead of the respiratory system) and the number of antigens injected at once, the immune system has no natural way of dealing with the result. A stressed, ill, or weakened animal's immune system may not develop the antibodies the vaccinations are supposed to create. Fibrosarcomas (cancerous tumors) frequently appear at vaccination sites. The puppy may develop distemper or another dis-ease now or later and the standard vet makes excuses or gives the disease another name. Many animals die this way.

Another result of vaccination is that the immune system, weakened and confused by the number of antigens it has been hit with all at once, goes awry and any number of new dis-eases may result. These are usually chronic dis-eases that appear early or late in the dog's life, seriously affecting the animal's quality of life and potential for good health. Some of these dis-eases in dogs include skin problems, auto-immune dis-eases including arthritis, spinal myelopathy, asthma, endocrine deficiencies, gum dis-ease, irritable bowel syndrome, and warts, growths, and tumors of all types. Lyme vaccine has significant side effects including arthritis and lockjaw. Rabies vaccinations, required yearly by law in most states, though immunity continues much longer (possibly for life), cause the worst reactions. These include irritability, personality changes, skin dis-ease, thyroid and endocrine dysfunctions, seizures, and immune system breakdowns including cancer.

This is not new information. Homeopaths have described and warned against vaccination failure and vaccinosis (dis-ease states caused by vaccination) since before 1900. The first vaccine, developed for smallpox by Jenner in 1796, was the point where homeopathy and allopathic medicine first seriously diverged. Once smallpox vaccination was instituted in England the usual few hundred cases a year escalated to many thousands of smallpox deaths. This repeated in other countries where statistics were kept and the deaths were nearly all by people who had been vaccinated. When mass vaccinations were terminated, smallpox declined drastically in every country that stopped them. This phenomenon has been repeated from country to country for a variety of dis-eases, including more currently polio and measles. While animal death statistics have not been kept as they have for humans, the pattern seems to repeat in animal and dog dis-eases of all sorts.[1]

What became clear to nineteenth-century homeopaths is again becoming clear to holistic veterinarians: that vaccination does not protect against the dis-eases it claims to, but instead creates a consistent pattern of serious, degenerative chronic dis-ease that may be lifelong and life threatening. Dr. Richard Pitcairn, pioneer in holistic veterinary procedures, shows the relationship of chronic dis-ease to the acute dis-ease the vaccination is meant to protect against. In his arti-cle "A New Look at the Vaccine Question," he describes the symptoms of acute canine distemper and rabies and compares them to the chronic symptoms of dis-temper and rabies vaccinosis.

The comparisons are striking. A dog with distemper shows the following symptoms: watery discharge from eyes and nose, conjunctivitis, vomiting and severe diarrhea with watery, bloody and odorous feces, loss of appetite and weight, lethargy, spasms and seizures, paralysis, rashes around mouth and abdomen, swollen feet and red pads, pneumonia, wasting away, and death. The chronic vaccinosis reactions to distemper vaccination are drippy nose, chronic runny eyes and conjunctivitis, chronic digestive and appetite disorders, hepati-tis, pancreatitis, parvovirus, chronic or recurrent diarrhea, food sensitivities resulting in diarrhea, epilepsy, spondylitis, rear leg paralysis, rashes around mouth and abdomen, rashes and inflammations of toes and feet, kennel cough and chronic bronchitis, abnormal thinness, and failure to thrive. Some or all the

1 Dr. Richard Pitcairn, DVM, Ph.D., "A New Look at the Vaccine Question," Eugene, Oregon, *Animal Natural Health*, undated article, p. 10-11.

symptoms of the original acute dis-ease manifest in a chronic way in animals vaccinated for distemper.[2]

The chronic manifestations of rabies vaccination show a similar and even more worrisome pattern. The symptoms for rabies vaccinosis include restlessness, suspiciousness, the desire to kill other animals, aggression, change of behavior, clingy behavior, hysteria or violence when restrained, self-mutilation, over-barking in a hoarse voice, finicky appetite, partial paralysis of mouth (drooling, sloppy eaters), visual defects and dis-eases, eating strange things including feces, destructive behavior, seizures, epilepsy, chorea, sexual aggression, heart failure and irregular pulse, and "reverse" sneezing/wheezing attacks.[3] Add immune breakdown (say cancer) and the above two examples are a catalog of all the things humans and dogs are dying of in this modern medical age. How many people understand that the medical system has created these sufferings?

Many of the dis-eases appear or reappear just after the yearly vaccinations. Tiger received her first rabies shot at four months old; she received all her shots early as she had been weaned very early. She was teething at that time and developed a fever and her adult teeth came in without enamel. They were brown and soft, broke easily, and developed many cavities. Copper received bordatella immunization upon insistence from his boarding kennel. I left him there for a weekend two weeks later and he came home with bordatella. When I took him back to the standard veterinarian I was using at the time, the "cure" was another immunization. Bordatella is self-limiting in about two weeks and the dog had it for two weeks. An all-too-typical story is of a dog developing tumors. "She was fine last month," the dog's person says, "we were at the vet's then for vaccinations."

Holistic Alternatives to Vaccinations

So what to do? Routine vaccinations are supposed to protect our puppies and dogs from some very nasty dis-eases but the protection itself is unreliable and causes more serious dis-ease. Is there any alternative? Your holistic veterinarian can offer a protocol of homeopathic nosodes alone or combined with far fewer standard injections. This is half of the answer. Antidoting the allopathic

2 Ibid., p. 5-6.
3 Ibid., p. 7-8.

vaccination side effects with homeopathic remedies is the other half. A nosode is a homeopathic vaccination, a usually harmless and highly diluted form of a killed dis-ease product specially prepared. Some holistic veterinarians use only nosodes in immunization. Others administer one or two of the puppy shots then do the boosters by nosode. Homeopathic immunization develops the necessary protection. It is reliable, and without short- or long-term side effects. Holistic veterinarians use the nosodes, allopathic veterinarians do not. Nosodes are also available from homeopathic laboratories and with a little understanding of the method can be easily given at home.

Different practitioners use different protocols for these vaccinations but most holistic vets use Dr. Richard Pitcairn's protocol. Dr. Pitcairn uses a nosode combination for dogs that includes distemper, parvovirus, bordatella, leptospirosis, and rabies; he uses this in ascending potencies of 30C, 200C and 1M. The remedies are liquid combinations placed on the dog's tongue. Food and water are withheld for about half an hour after giving them. Begin with the 30C potency administered one dose each week for three treatments, then wait two weeks. Next go to the 200C potency, giving one dose every three weeks for a total of three treatments. Wait for one month, then give one dose of 1M potency nosodes, repeating it every four months for life.[4] The nosodes may be ordered from the Newton Homeopathic Laboratories, or Hahnemann Pharmacy (see Resources for address).

Luc Chalton of Newton Laboratories offers another protocol. He suggests that a daily dose (3-6 drops) of the liquid canine nosode combination be given on three days of the first week, once a week for the next three weeks, once a month for the next six months, then once every six months after. If the animal has been exposed to a particular dis-ease or there is an epidemic of a canine dis-ease, give an additional nosode dose weekly. He notes that there are a variety of effective protocols for nosode use. The formula above can also be used to antidote the negative side effects of past allopathic injections. Nosodes can be used to prepare the immune system for standard vaccinations by starting them two days before the injections are given. Then follow the allopathic vaccinations with the nosode protocol.

4 Richard H. Pitcairn, DVM, Ph.D., "Homeopathic Alternatives to Vaccines," Eugene, OR, *Animal Natural Health*, undated article, p. 9.

Homeopathic veterinarian Wendy Thacher-Jensen, DVM, gives two allopathic puppy shots a month apart for parvovirus and distemper only. If the injections can be given separately, all the better. No other vaccinations for these dis-eases are needed for the life of the dog. For rabies, she vaccinates at four months then follows the legal requirements of her area. She does not vaccinate for kennel cough (bordatella) or lyme dis-ease. According to Dr. Ron Schultz, DVM, of the University of Wisconsin Veterinary School, the two puppy injections offer protection for at least twelve years; there is no need to re-vaccinate. Rabies vaccination may be adequate for life also; when the vaccine was developed testing was stopped at three years.

Blood titre checks can be done to prove antibody levels for all the vaccina-tion dis-eases and they will meet state licensing laws. To be accepted at boarding kennels you may ask the kennel operator for a release form or your holistic vet-erinarian can certify that the dog is protected. Dr. Jensen does not do antidote protocols if the dog is under any other treatment and prefers to treat each case constitutionally for the individual's highly specific needs.

Larry Bernstein, VMD, who is also a homeopathic veterinarian, prefers nosode immunization but some guardians still wish to vaccinate. In this case, he gives one allopathic injection to puppies at eight or nine weeks, and another at four and a half to five months. He uses the whole complex except leptospirosis and lyme vaccine (which cause significant reactions) and gives a rabies injection with the second series. He follows the injections with homeopathic antidotes— *Thuja*, *Silica*, or *Sulfur*, depending on the individual canine. To antidote the dan-gerous rabies after-effects he uses homeopathic *Thuja* before and *Lyssin* (rabies nosode) after in 30C or greater potency. He may also use homeopathic prepara-tions of *Belladonna*, *Stramonium*, or *Hyascamus* in place of *Lyssin*. At one year he goes to nosodes using Dr. Pitcairn's protocol.

He also employs the blood titre test, which costs about twenty dollars to prove protection and writes a release letter to boarding kennels. For adult dogs one further set of injections is optional to be followed by the antidotes. He states that the nosode for bordatella works more effectively than the standard immunization. For an older dog new to holistics who has been previously vaccinated yearly, Dr. Bernstein treats the animal constitutionally, suggests an optimal diet, and antidotes the vaccine side-effects as above. No more allopathic injections are given ever. Homeopathic *Nux Vomica* may be used for pets that have been over-medicated or homeopathic *Sulfur*.

Pharmacist Allen M. Kratz of HVS Laboratories manufactures combination homeopathic remedies for detoxification. His HomeoVetix preparations are available through veterinarians. To antidote the standard injections in adult dogs or puppies he has designed Virotox, one capful in water once a day for twenty-four days started immediately after vaccination. To minimize side effects before standard vaccinations are given, use Supportasode for twenty-four days before vaccinating and continue it for twenty-four days after. If your puppy or older dog has been previously raised on supermarket junk food, use HVS's Chemotox once a week along with Supportasode to detoxify the animal. He notes that if you do allopathic injections, only vaccinate a healthy puppy.

The above gives the pet guardian some alternatives and ideas. A woman once told me she was about to euthanize her eleven-year-old cat because he had developed tumors all over his body. The story was familiar. She had just had the cat vaccinated. I suggested she try homeopathic *Thuja* in 30C potency, giving a dose nightly for one week and then stop. The cat's tumors disappeared completely within two weeks. I have heard similar stories frequently. After losing Cinde, Tiger, and Dusty all to cancer, I needed to know why; bad food and vaccinations were clearly the cause. Copper and Kali are on holistic homeopathic protocols, and it is interesting to note an experience of my own. After taking only one dose of Newton Homeopathics' human Vaccination Complex, I developed detoxification symptoms and diarrhea for over a week. Everything you have read here about puppies and dogs applies to you and your children.

Holistic Treatments for Parasites

Holistic treatments are also available for intestinal parasites (worms). The general consensus of veterinarians I interviewed is that many puppies are born with roundworms but in a healthy puppy they will disappear untreated by six months of age. If the pup is not heavily infested and is otherwise without symptoms, and if she is on an optimal diet, you may leave them untreated. Wheat germ added to the diet (1/2 to 2 teaspoons daily) and raw garlic (1/2 to 2 grated cloves daily) will help to remove roundworms. Give 10,000 IU of vitamin A once a week and see the information below on diatomaceous earth. For tapeworms, Richard Pitcairn gives 1/4 to 1 teaspoonful of raw ground pumpkin seeds (unsalted) per meal and the same amount of wheat germ oil. He uses papaya enzymes or a digestive enzyme combination from a health food store in the same amounts as the wheat germ and pumpkin seeds. The homeopathic remedy for roundworms is *Cina*, and for tapeworms *Felix mas*. Give an occasional castor oil laxative after a day of fasting to remove the weakened worms.[5]

Diatomaceous earth, also called fossil flour, is the remains of a sea plankton. Its minute skeletal shell cuts through single-celled organisms and is a major irritant to other microscopic life. It will not harm a mammal when used internally or externally. Externally, diatomaceous earth is used as a totally nontoxic flea powder. It may be also be used internally in dogs and puppies as a worming agent. Buy it at health food stores—do not use the diatomaceous earth used for swimming pools—and mix 1/4 to two teaspoonsful in your puppy or dog's food. Give it daily for a week then wait a week and repeat three times. It is effective for all types of worms and may also be used as a heartworm preventive once a week. Some holistic vets are cautious of this, but it works.

Prince, an adult Shetland sheepdog, tried diatomaceous earth. Since his adoption, Prince has been chronically underweight despite good food. Though I've suspected worms they did not show up in a fecal check and his person decided to try the remedy. By the end of the first week's trial of diatomaceous earth Prince started gaining weight and has filled out considerably and rapidly. There have been no adverse reactions of any kind.

The holistic veterinarians I interviewed for this book both use standard chemical injections for worms, Nemex or Strongid once or twice and Droncit for tapeworms. They feel this is easier than natural treatment and the chemicals

5 Richard H. Pitcairn, DVM, Ph.D. and Susan Hubble Pitcairn, *Dr. Pitcairn's Complete Guide to Natural Health for Dogs and Cats*, (Emmaus, PA, Rodale Press, 1995), p. 330-333.

cause no harm. The vets recommend the allopathic monthly Heartgard for heart-worm prevention, noting that in cold climates it does not have to be given in the winter. Heartgard can be given every forty-five days instead of monthly and they feel it is safe for healthy puppies and dogs.

Dr. Jensen treats heartworm infections only; she does not use the preventive and uses black walnut tincture, vitamin C, and the dog's homeopathic constitu-tional remedy for treatment. Dr. Bernstein uses the standard preventive for healthy animals. For heartworm dis-ease treatment, he uses the same remedies as Dr. Jensen does and adds pumpkin seeds to it. Note that Dr. Bernstein's practice is in Florida, where mosquitoes are a year-round problem, and Dr. Jensen's prac-tice is further north. They generally agree that a healthy dog will have fewer or no parasites inside or out.

The information of this chapter differs greatly from what people are used to hearing from allopathic veterinarians and allopathic medicine. I can tell you only that it works, that I use these methods for my dogs and recommend them for yours. An animal or human that employs natural methods of diet and health care lives a longer, better life. The next chapter offers some further natural remedies for puppies and dogs.

some natural remedies

The more you work with holistic methods of wellness and healing, the more you will want to. They are effective, and they cause no discomfort or harm. They put health care back into our hands and give parents and pet guardians an alternative and choice. Holistic healing is designed to keep people and animals well and to prevent small dis-eases from becoming big ones. While it is not the answer to every ill, it is the answer to most of them. The more you learn about natural methods and use them, the more you will be able to do for yourself and your dog. In this chapter, I will offer a few suggestions for using natural remedies for adult dogs and puppies.

Acquiring and Administering Homeopathic, Herbal, and Organic Remedies

You will find most of your natural remedies in health food stores. (I mean stores dedicated to human health.) The remedies are the same for pets as for people. On the bottles instructions are given for a human adult of about a hundred and fifty pounds. In general, based on the dog or puppy's weight, give a fraction of the human dosage. For a fifteen- to thirty-pound dog or puppy the amount is about a quarter of the human dose, from thirty to seventy pounds half the human dose, and for a larger dog about three quarters of the human recommendation. A puppy that needs digestive enzymes would probably be given a quarter of a tablet. For younger puppies or very small puppies, get children's supplements and figure size and weight requirements from those labels. There are many pediatric vitamins available in liquid form. Look for supplements designed for pets, but know that human ones are safe as long as the dose is divided for the puppy or dog's size.

Your dog can use any human remedy with a couple of exceptions. Aspirin or aspirin substitutes like willow bark should not be used often on a grown dog and not on small puppies at all. (For cats, even a single dose of aspirin can be fatal.) Remedies with alcohol bases should be diluted or the alcohol evaporated by placing the drops in hot water before giving them to the animal. This may be done for herb tinctures but not for flower essences or homeopathic remedies. Heat will inactivate these remedies but the alcohol in them is minimal anyway and you will give your pet only a few drops. Herbal tinctures are given by the drop and you will use only about three drops per dose for a small puppy, five drops for a dog under thirty pounds and ten drops for a large-breed adult. The dosage is far less critical than with chemical drugs and a few drops more will cause no harm.

For homeopathic remedies or flower essences the same dose is given for an elephant or a mouse—or a human, a grown dog, or a puppy. Information on how to administer pellet remedies was given in the grooming and handling chapter. Place a few (4 to 6) pellets crushed or whole, into the dog or puppy's mouth. If some of the powder or pellets drop to the floor, don't worry about it and don't try to pick them up. As long as some of the remedy gets in, the dog has received the dose. With liquid homeopathic preparations place a few drops into the animal's mouth; three to six drops will do it. The dosage is the same for flower essences. Homeopathic remedies come in potencies described in the last chapter. For home use I recommend using 30C potencies but your health food store may only carry 6X. What to do? Where a 30C potency is given only once a day, a 6X potency is given more often. Avoid using potencies higher than 30C unless you are experienced in homeopathy or are expressly directed to by the vaccination protocols or your homeopathic veterinarian.

How often do you give a remedy? With an herb tincture add the dosage to each mealtime, mixed with food. Give flower essences one to three times a day, but not along with food or other remedies. Vitamin supplements are usually based on a daily dose that you can give in one meal or divide up among the day's meals. If your puppy is taking digestive enzymes give them with each meal. Your holistic veterinarian will tell you how often to give the homeopathic remedies she prescribes. If you use them without veterinary direction the frequency you decide on should be based on observation of your pet.

With homeopathy it is crucial to give the right remedy for the dog or puppy's symptoms. Each remedy is a picture of the symptom, and if your pet's symptoms don't quite match the remedy may not work at all. If nothing changes after a couple of tries with a remedy you have the wrong one. This is what makes homeopathy so much of a challenge and can make it frustrating for beginners. A good guide book goes a long way to help you choose the right remedy the first time. If you use a 30C potency give the remedy once and then stop. Watch your pet over the next few hours to see her reaction. Have her symptoms lessened or worsened? Has she had any change in behavior or habit?

For example, when I gave Copper a dose of *Phosphorus* 12C (a lower potency than 30C) that saved his life, he went to sleep for hours and that was different from his usual habit. His diarrhea and vomiting completely stopped. If the symptoms have stopped or are improving you don't need to continue the remedy. When his symptoms started again ten days later, Copper got his second dose. His symptoms the second time were much less severe than before the first dose—there was obvious improvement. Chronic dis-eases may take a longer time to improve; give your 30C dose once a day for a few days and then stop and wait. If you see improvement, give no more doses until the symptoms return or get worse. These directions are the same for lower potencies but with an X potency the action lasts a much shorter time. Watch your pet's behavior and you will know when to repeat the remedy.

What if her symptoms worsen after giving a remedy? This can happen occasionally and is not cause for alarm. Sometimes the right remedy will cause an aggravation, which means a temporary speeding up or worsening of the symptoms, though the animal's general energy is improved. On a 30C or greater potency you may see this but you probably will not on a lower potency. You should understand that an aggravation is considered positive because it means that you have correctly matched your remedy to the dog or puppy's dis-ease. Aggravations rarely last longer than a couple of hours and once they stop the improvement will be rapid. If your pet's symptoms get worse, wait to give any further dose until the aggravation and the improvement that follows end.

Every homeopath has her chosen potencies and while one may work exclusively with 30C and say nothing lower is worth bothering with, another gets optimal results on 10X or 15X. All of it works; follow your practitioner's directions for whatever potency she prefers. Homeopaths also work under two schools and a practitioner who holds to one will often reject the other. The differences may be more philosophical than medical. The issue of disagreement is between single remedies and combinations. Single remedy homeopathy, classical homeopathy, is used by many holistic veterinarians. Combination remedies also work and work well—I use them on myself and on my animals. In a homeopathic combination your usually liquid remedy will be labeled for a specific condition instead of naming a single remedy.

Combination remedies for pets include the combined nosodes mentioned in the last chapter. Some other combination remedies available for dogs are: Flea and Bug Bites, Eye Irritation, Bowel Discomfort, Skin Relief, Rheumatic Pain, Worms and Parasites, and Kidney and Bladder Relief. The vaccination detoxifiers from HomeoVetix described in the last chapter are also combination remedies. These are administered differently from most homeopathic preparations in that a capful is placed in the dog's water once a day. Though some classical homeopaths disparage combination remedies, they often work beautifully. They are wonderful for people new to homeopathy who care less about philosophy and more about quick results.

One other type of remedy you will occasionally use for puppies and dogs is external. These are salves or antiseptics placed on the skin for healing wounds, sores, and skin lesions. Herbal salves work well but can rub off on your carpets and furniture and make a mess. I personally prefer herbal tinctures and a few drugstore items that are sprayed or dripped on and do not stain once dry. Your pet will lick them off so they must be safe and remain effective even after your pet tries to lick them off. A dog with external sores usually needs internal medication as well. Often the same herb or herb combination can be used internally and externally. For example, for skin sores I spray a combination of comfrey and goldenseal tinctures externally and place drops of the same combination in the pet's food. Besides being a powerful herbal antibiotic and antiseptic, goldenseal tastes so bad that most dogs will not lick it off. External remedies have no dosage: just spray, drip or smear them on.

One further type of external remedy is aromatherapy or essential oils. These are highly concentrated plant extracts often used as insect repellents for pets. A few drops of aromatherapy oils can be added to shampoos for effective flea control. Except for lavender or tea tree oils they are always diluted, usually in water or in a mild carrier oil. Lavender or tea tree oil can be used directly as antiseptics on skin lesions. These oils are used by the drop. They are never given for internal use.

Natural Remedies for Fleas

The first natural remedies I want to discuss in this chapter are for fleas. It is extremely important to learn holistic methods for flea prevention and for relief of flea bites. Chemical flea products do untold harm causing cancer and immune disorders, kidney failure, liver damage, skin rashes and permanent hair loss, birth defects, heavy metal poisoning, leukemia, nervous system damage, seizures, lung problems, vomiting, allergies, and behavior problems. When these chemicals are on your dog or in your home they are harming you as well. The worst offenders are flea collars, which are made from the same chemicals as the nerve gases used in World War II. No matter how much you poison and bomb the fleas they will still return, and moreover your pet and your family are being poisoned.

I live in Florida, flea capitol of the planet, and experience fleas on my heavy coated dogs less than once a year and usually for periods of less than a week. How? First of all, my animals are fed an optimal diet, which makes them healthy and resistant to all invasions. They are given no chemicals of any kind to deplete their natural immune systems and I allow no chemicals to be used in my yard or garden. Second, with each meal (they eat once a day) I feed five tablets of brewer's yeast with garlic. These are available in powder or tablet form at any standard pet supplier and though the dosage states one tablet per ten pounds body weight slightly less works for me. (Kali weighs around fifty-five pounds and Copper seventy-five). The tablets cost ten dollars for a thousand. You can also use nutritional yeast from a health food store. Give a teaspoonful of nutritional or brewer's yeast daily for small dogs and puppies and a tablespoonful for a fifty-pound dog. The flea-repelling effects take about a month to kick in and you must feed the yeast daily and reliably for the effects to continue.

My house is treated yearly by a natural exterminating company. My rugs, furniture, in the rafters and under appliances, are dusted with a combination of boric acid, borax, magnesium stearate, and diatomaceous earth. The treatment is so safe that neither I nor the dogs need to leave the premises while it's being done or after. If fleas are still a problem my yard can be treated with a sprayed solution of beneficial nematodes and the problem ends. I have experienced liver damage from standard chemical exterminating since I've lived in Florida and am grateful for the alternative, as exterminating is as routine as another utility in this hot climate. I have no problem with fleas and also no problem with the tapeworms that fleas carry. If my dogs show sign of fleas a bath in blue dishwashing liquid is usually enough.

If there are fleas on your dog there are ten times as many in your home. The following home recipe, based on the professional formula, works. Use half a cup each of boric acid or borax (or both), salt, and diatomaceous earth. Diatomaceous earth is available at health food stores or from the catalogs listed in the Resource section. Boric acid comes from drug stores and borax from the supermarket laundry section. Beneficial nematodes for flea control are available from pet suppliers or from organic gardening centers.

Diatomaceous earth without the other ingredients can be used safely as a flea powder on even the youngest puppies. Other herbal flea powders that can be used in your home and on your puppy or dog include powdered bulk herbs of bay, eucalyptus, pennyroyal, rosemary, rue, or wormwood. These can be mixed with pyrethrum powder or diatomaceous earth as both flea killers and repellents.[1] To use these combinations in your home sprinkle them liberally on your rugs, under and on upholstery and under appliances, in cupboards and into all cracks and corners of the rooms. Work the powders into your rugs with a clean broom and leave them on at least overnight before vacuuming. Repeat the application monthly or as needed. In cold climates the fleas disappear around November and do not return until spring; do one more application then stop until warm weather.

Aromatherapy essential oils may also be used as repellents but may not be strong enough to kill fleas. Use half a teaspoonful of basil, bay, citronella, eucalyptus, lavender, pennyroyal, rosemary, or thyme oil in a pint of water in a spray bottle.[2] Soak the dog's coat—the oils smell wonderful—but avoid the eyes. These oils are only safe when they are diluted. An excellent prepared combination of essential oils is Critter Oil (see Resources). This is made of essential oils of lemon, cedarwood, grapefruit, pennyroyal, eucalyptus, and sage. In different mixes it makes a wonderful, skin-soothing flea spray for pet or home and a shampoo that leaves your dog's coat flea free and smelling great. There is no need to use chemicals for fleas.

Natural Remedies for Ear Infections and Ear Mites

Ear infections and ear mites are another common problem that pet guardians face. If your dog allows you to handle her, you may be able to treat this at home. Copper came to me with infected ears and the infections recurred repeatedly until I changed him to preservative-free food. In seven years he has only had one more infection, probably from water in his ears during bathing.

When I was grooming dogs, every cocker spaniel that came to me had chronically infected ears; the long ear flaps prevent air from getting in and drying the ear canal. For dogs with hair inside the ear canal opening, like cockers and

1 Janette Grainger and Connie Moore, *Natural Insect Repellents for Pets, People and Plants*, (Austin, TX, The Herb Bar, 1991), p. 16.
2 Ibid., p. 12-13.

poodles, it is best to pull the hair out. Dogs seldom protest this and your groomer can show you how. Afterwards wipe the inside of the ear with a cotton ball soaked in peroxide, witch hazel, or echinacea tincture. When you are bathing your dog, place oiled cotton balls in her ears to prevent water getting in and making infection conditions possible. Most of these infections are fungal. If you use antibiotics, your dog will be even more susceptible to such infections—another reason for holistic veterinary treatment.

An infected ear has a brown sticky or grainy discharge, may look inflamed, and has a musty odor. The infection can be caused by candida albicans or other fungus, a parasite called ear mites, or an object like a plant seed in the ear. Foreign objects usually require veterinary extraction but may work free with the following treatment. Remember that a puppy or dog fed on preservative-free food and whose natural immune response has not been compromised by chemicals and vaccinations is far less likely to develop any kind of dis-ease or parasites including ear infections.

Start by cleaning the ears with a cotton ball and antiseptic. Do not use cotton swabs as you may injure the delicate organs. Wet the cotton ball with any of the following: hydrogen peroxide, rubbing alcohol, apple cider vinegar, diluted betadine, echinacea tincture, witch hazel, or aloe vera juice with peroxide. One standard veterinarian uses half hydrogen peroxide and half alcohol undiluted. It may take several cotton balls until all the discharge is removed. Clean both ears. Your dog may balk at the attention, as infected ears are uncomfortable and painful, but the cleaning is necessary.

Once this is done you may also fill the ear canal with an eyedropper of aloe vera juice and hydrogen peroxide (make the mix with two ounces of aloe vera juice or gel and a teaspoonful of three-percent hydrogen peroxide). Massage the base of the ears to get the liquid well in (it will sound squishy) and then let the dog shake the rest out (try and stop her!). You may also do this with undiluted echinacea tincture, alcohol based only. Clean the ears and treat them in this way daily until no more discharge appears and the ears are clean and without inflammation. It may take a week to ten days.

After cleaning the ears, on alternate days squeeze the fluid from a couple of vitamin E capsules into the ear canal. Puncture the capsules with a clean pin or needle to open them. You can use mullein and garlic ear oil which is available in health food stores, or plain garlic oil, or rosemary tincture, or strong rosemary tea added to olive oil. Make sure that there are no pieces of herb in the oil. You can also add five drops of rosemary, tea tree, or lavender essential oil to a half ounce of olive oil. Alternating the ear cleaning with the oils may release a foreign object in the ear, as it did once for Kali, and is good for smothering ear mites.

Homeopathy for ear infections can include *Hepar sulph* when the ear is very inflamed and sensitive. You can use *Graphites* for ears that have a lot of smelly discharge. If the dog or puppy exhibits great pain in her reaction to your touching her ears try *Chamomilla*; this is a particularly useful remedy for puppies of teething age. If the earflap and canal look wet, sore, and red, the remedy is *Merc sol*. If the puppy seems restless, worse at night, and has a watery ear discharge use *Arsenicum*. Flower essences for ear infections may include Essential Essences Detox or Blood Cleansing Essence, or Bach's Crab Apple. If the dog is in much distress either from the infection or from your treatment give her Rescue Remedy, Calming Essence, or Essential Essence's Pet Rescue Combination. See your holistic veterinarian if the infection does not clear within two weeks.

Natural Remedies for Diarrhea

Diarrhea is another common difficulty puppy guardians meet at one time or another. It is a symptom rather than a dis-ease and in older puppies and dogs can usually be traced to something they have eaten. In a very young puppy a serious case of diarrhea can be life threatening because of dehydration; if it continues past four hours contact your holistic vet. Diarrhea can come from but is less serious when it accompanies teething, when you have introduced a new food, or have given her too much fruit or vegetables, cow's milk, or vitamin C. It can also come from eating garbage or inedible items, eating grass, or while expelling worms (they are better expelled than inside). Sometimes rawhide bones are a source of either diarrhea or constipation. Some breeds of puppies tend to have chronically loose stools that are not actually diarrhea. This is true of Siberian Huskies. The condition corrects itself as the puppy gets older.

A puppy or dog on preservative-free food who is not exposed to toxins and whose vaccinations are natural or have been antidoted is the least likely to have chronic diarrhea problems. If your puppy has diarrhea frequently, reduce her vitamin C intake and start her on a quarter of a tablet of digestive enzymes with each meal. Have her checked for worms by taking a fresh stool sample to your veterinarian and by observing whether round worms (they looked coiled like spaghetti) or tapeworms (they look like grains of rice) are present. If she has eaten something nasty, fast her for a meal or two while her intestines clean out.

Offer plenty of fresh water at all times and add a teaspoonful of organic apple cider vinegar to the water to restore electrolytes and prevent dehydration. Or add a tablespoonful of organic apple juice plus a tablespoon of raw honey or a tablespoonful of liquid chlorophyll per pint of water. Pedialyte for infants may also be placed in the water bowl to prevent dehydration. You can find it displayed in a supermarket with the baby products. You can feed her a teaspoonful of liquid acidophilus to restore beneficial bowel bacteria.

Some herbs and herbal teas are binding. Slippery elm powder (Juliette Levy's tree barks powder) mixed with raw honey forms a paste that tastes good to puppies and will soothe their stomachs; it will also get puppies to eat if nothing else will. Make and cool strong blackberry tea; the tea bags are available in supermarkets. Feed the puppy a few teaspoonsful. Add a pinch of cinnamon to either of these as it is sweet and stops diarrhea. Cooled chamomile tea is optimal for teething age puppies, and is also readily available.

The homeopathic combination I prefer for puppies is *Chamomilla* with *Podophyllum*. Give the first remedy and wait ten minutes before giving the second. Wait for a response before you give any more. For puppies with chronic diarrhea you may give a 30C dose of each of these once a day for a few days. It may stop the diarrhea permanently. Try it for three days, then stop for three days. If diarrhea returns give it for three days again. *Chamomilla* is a remedy that may benefit teething age puppies with almost any dis-ease. *Podophyllum* is used for diarrhea after eating fruit or too much vitamin C. *Nux Vomica* is the remedy for garbage can raiders.

Arsenicum is used when diarrhea is accompanied by vomiting that may be frequent; the dog is restless and feels cold to the touch. She is thirsty but vomits back the water. For frequent diarrhea with straining but no vomiting try *Merc cor.* Copious, chronic, debilitating diarrhea responds to *Phosphorus*, but in this case see your holistic veterinarian. For an angry, irritable dog or puppy with diarrhea and colic use *Colocynthis*. Frequent watery diarrhea responds to *Croton tig.*

Flower essences that may help include Rescue Remedy, Calming Essence, or Essential Essence's Pet Rescue Combination. Detoxification essences like Essential Essence's Detox Essence or Bach's Crab Apple are also useful.

Do not allow diarrhea to continue for long in a puppy without contacting your veterinarian, and if there is blood in the stool seek help immediately. At any age, do not wait until your animal becomes debilitated before seeking expert help. The remedies above will stop most simple diarrhea that is not from dis-ease. Puppies will eat almost anything and leave their people to deal with the consequences. This is another good reason to puppy-proof your home and keep unsafe things out of reach, but a dog's ingenuity at eating things you would never think of will astound you.

Older dogs that get into garbage suffer the consequences, too. Dusty got loose once and visited every garbage can in the neighborhood before I caught up with her. She was sick for days and deserved it. She also made a habit of going through my backpack and visitors' suitcases to eat such things as vitamins and toothpaste. Tiger liked to chew on wall plaster and was probably calcium deficient. A dog that eats her own feces, a trait called coprophagia, is also deficient in minerals and other nutrition. Pets on natural food are far less likely to eat strange things but some are simply greedy.

Appendix I offers a list of very brief uses for some common homeopathic remedies. This chapter has offered only a beginning discussion of holistic remedies and healing. There are many excellent books on the market to continue your learning and I recommend your doing so.

four-footed teenagers from hell

Suddenly your puppy isn't a baby any more. She's big and gawky and your sweet little angel is a terror. She pretends she doesn't know you when you call her or she doesn't remember her name. She seems to have forgotten all the obedience training you thought she'd long since learned. She runs through the house knocking things over, steals food, and sleeps on the couch (or eats it) when you're not at home. You thought she was house-trained but is she? You don't think this could happen to you with your darling puppy? It will. It starts around six months of age and may last a year. If your dog is a Siberian maniac it may last several years. Eventually your puppy will wake up and remember who she is. She'll grow up but it'll take awhile. Be prepared, hold on, and don't give up.

When to Spay or Neuter Your Pet

Spaying or neutering needs to be done by this age if it hasn't been done sooner. This is necessary for any dog that is a pet; leave breeding to the knowledgeable breeders of top-quality show dogs. There are thousands upon thousands of other pure and mixed-breed dogs, all loving souls, that need homes desperately, too many to make breeding an ethical alternative. Your children don't need to see a litter. You can show them a video or take them to a kennel for such education. Eighty to one hundred million dogs and cats are born in the United States yearly, two to three thousand per hour, many more than can ever find homes. Thirteen and a half million animals are euthanized per year.[1] Do the right thing and spay or neuter your pet.

The surgery should be done before a teenage puppy's secondary sex characteristics begin to assert themselves. A female at six months comes into her first season, which resembles human menstruation. The season or heat lasts three weeks and happens twice a year. Her spotting will stain your rugs and furniture, she will develop an odor, and her condition will draw every unneutered male dog for five miles around to your doorstep. The males will bark, howl, and stage fights with each other. They will obstruct and challenge you when you leave your house, with or without your dog. From the tenth to fourteenth day of her season your female is fertile and will make every attempt to be mated. Instinct and desperation make dogs escape artists at this time and a fenced yard is not enough. Your puppy will get out or the males will get in. Does your six-month-old need to be a mother? Spaying before the first heat prevents all this and may also prevent breast cancer when she is older. The raging hormones are no joy to her and she will be happier for the surgery.

With males you have other problems, like spraying in the house, running off, and acting belligerent. He is not forgetting house-training—he is marking your home as his territory. The message is not only for other dogs, but for you, too. A teenage male dog in a dog pack begins to assert his place in the adult pecking order. He would like to be pack leader and instinct requires him to try for the job. In your family-pack, however, you are the leader and his ambition is mistaken. He is also maturing sexually and may mount people and other animals in the home. Discipline this with a firm "no, off." If a female within five miles is in season your unneutered male will answer the call. He too becomes an escape artist

1 Monks of New Skete, *How to Be Your Dog's Best Friend: A Training Manual for Dog Owners*, (Boston, New York, Toronto and London, Little Brown and Co., 1978), p. 182.

and will go out to fight other male dogs and mate whatever females he can. Neutering before these characteristics develop makes your boy much happier. He then will not develop the need to challenge your leadership, to mount and behave sexually, to run away, fight other dogs, or spray in your home. A grown male dog lifts his leg to urinate but this is different from spraying and is normal.

Veterinarians have different opinions of when spaying and neutering should best take place. Some animal shelters do the surgery on puppies before adoption as young as eight weeks. Even six to eight weeks old is considered okay to do it. Dr. Wendy Thacher-Jensen says that the surgery is less of a shock to younger puppies than to older ones. They are under anesthetic for a shorter period of time and the new forms of anesthesia in use today are safer. She says that puppies neutered this young are less aggressive than those that have been neutered as adults.

Larry Bernstein, VMD, prefers to spay or neuter at six to nine months before the female's first heat and before the male begins to spray. He feels that the dog needs to be more mature as the surgery is major and has some anesthesia risk. The time when a very young puppy leaves its mother and comes to a new home is a time of high stress. Many puppies do not arrive in new homes in optimal condition and it's best to build their health before spaying or neutering. Other vets choose to neuter males as soon as the testicles drop at five to seven months and spay females at five months before the first heat. I prefer the last suggestion of about five months. If your female is in heat you must wait until her season ends to spay her and most veterinarians will not spay her if she is pregnant.

The Importance of Obedience Training

While behavior problems and wildness are helped and somewhat prevented by spaying and neutering they will not go away. A teenager is a teenager even if she is a dog. Your training methods must become more intensified in response to teenage behavior and your discipline may have to be more firm. This still does not permit you to hit your dog or to be cruel in any way. Your puppy has not forgotten everything she ever knew, she is testing you. She wants to know if you are still her pack leader and you must assure her that you are, by not allowing her to be disobedient. Six months is the time for formal obedience training and is your primary solution. I recommend it whole-heartedly.

Look in the telephone book for dog trainers or dog training schools and find out when a basic obedience class is starting. Some classes accept only purebred dogs while others accept all, purebred and mixed breeds. Your local humane society probably offers obedience classes, which are often held in a public park. Whether your dog is purebred or mixed-breed is irrelevant, she still needs obedience training. The classes usually last for ten weeks. They are held once a week and the cost can be as little as twenty-five dollars. Your biggest investment will not be money but time. Between the weekly classes you will need to do two training sessions a day with your dog, lasting fifteen or twenty minutes each. These sessions will determine how much you and your dog will get from the classes. Putting the work in now will make a difference in your dog's behavior for the rest of her life.

Too many people write off their dogs at six to nine months old because their wild behavior makes them impossible to live with. Too many dogs end up in shelters and die because their people didn't know about obedience training or didn't want to make the effort. A few weeks' hard work is required from you and your dog to give you both a lifetime of love and joy together. Make the effort and enter your puppy in an obedience class and do the necessary training yourself. The classes themselves and the experience shared with a group of other people and animals is great fun. Choose an obedience class that is not too large for individual attention and problem solving and where the trainer is willing to give such attention. Choose a trainer who works humanely at all times, that never hits an animal, and that does not resort to methods like "hanging" a misbehaving dog by her collar and leash. You will not want an instructor who uses the Koehler Method. Humor is important also.

When I began puppy obedience with Kali I discovered very quickly that a standard obedience correction, which if done properly is not cruel or violent, sends her into a snarling rage. She seems to have had some training since she understood the commands but her reaction was more than disturbing. The trainer suggested that she may have been abused and I talked to Kali psychically to find out. She showed me a picture of a large man hanging her off the ground by a single piece leash that ended in a loop for the slip collar. She was strangled and terrified and the person was not the one who raised her. Such leashes are often used by kennels, veterinarians, and shelters and are themselves are no problem. The hanging seems to have happened repeatedly. Kali was not going to allow it again. Obedience training with her was more than difficult. At six years of age she will now permit me to use standard obedience methods if I use them very gently. She is only now learning to trust me.

You will need a steel-linked training collar (choke collar or slip collar) that fits your dog properly and a six foot cloth training leash. The collar fits if, when tightened on your dog's neck, two or three inches of chain remain between your dog and the leash. You do not need, and should not use without expert guidance, a pinch collar with protruding prongs. They may have their place with adult dogs that are constant pullers but they must be used correctly. The right way to use a training collar is with the dog on your left side in heel position. The section attached to the leash rides over the dog's neck, not under her chin. The collar should pop and tighten when the leash is jerked and then release immediately.

You will hold the six-foot leash in both hands with it running across your body. A cloth leash is necessary as a chain one will hurt your hands and most obedience schools prefer a cotton leash to a nylon webbed one. Your first obedience class will show you the right way to use the training collar and leash. This is a new type of collar for your dog, so before classes begin to accustom her to it as you did to her flat collar when she was a baby. Take it on and off a few times and distract her if she fusses. Praise her. Never leave a training collar on while you are not training your dog, even if she is in her crate. The rings can catch on things and strangle her to death.

In a basic obedience class you and your dog will be taught to heel, sit, sit and stay, lie down, lie down and stay, and to come. The "come" command is taught last, as it is the most important. Your dog is first given experience in obeying you before it is taught. If you have followed the small puppy exercises described in earlier chapters, your teenager will not be difficult to train. The classes and home

Using a Training Collar[2]

2 Ibid., p. 130.

Holding the Leash[3]

3 Ibid., p. 175.

practice sessions will help to bond you with your pet. They will also remind your wayward child that you are still the boss and leader of the family-pack. If there is to be peace in your home for the next dozen years, if you are not to give up and ship your puppy elsewhere, maybe to her death, this learning is essential. I will not try to describe or teach the obedience curriculum but will leave it to experts. It is better to enter a qualified training class than to teach your dog from a book, especially if you have never done so before.

Some people and dogs find obedience training a joy and a fascination. They may enter show ring competition in obedience if their dog is a registered pure-bred. For purebred dogs in competition the first obedience degree is the CD title, Companion Dog. The next advanced degree is the CDX—Companion Dog Excellent, with more demanding requirements on dog and handler. The UD (Utility Dog) degree is next and if your dog passes tracking requirements she may earn the UDT degree, Utility Dog Tracking. There are also degrees in Agility. Few dogs go this far. Pure or mixed-breed dogs can compete for the Canine Good Citizen (CGC degree) which is now often required for service dogs who work in nursing homes and hospitals. Your first basic obedience class can open up a whole new world. Some dog breeds take more readily to obedience training than do others, but all dogs benefit from it.

If you adopted a grown dog she may have surprises for you. Obedience training is the time when old learning comes home to roost for good or ill. You may have to do some retraining (as I did with Kali) or live with your dog's bad old habits. You may also find that your dog knows the ropes already. When Copper went to class with Kali the instructor chose him for a model on the first day, perhaps because he was older than most of his six-month-old classmates. Copper with great dignity preceded through the entire obedience routine one step ahead of the instructor's commands. He apparently had done it before and was quite proud of his performance. The problem was that once he had done it he wouldn't continue his good work. "I showed you I could do it, didn't I?" he said. "I don't have to do it again." He absolutely refuses to sit outdoors when heeling though will do so inside. When I ask him why he tells me, "hot

holistic puppy

sidewalk." I guess I can't complain. The dog is well-behaved for home living if not for competition.

Methods of Halting Obnoxious and Destructive Behavior

Along with obedience training you may need some help with problem solving. Your obedience instructor has answers to some of the four-footed teenager-from-hell behaviors you will go through at this time. Cayenne pepper for the inveterate food stealer or beggar is one such solution. Using a startle can or chain is another. These techniques are not for small puppies but a teenage smart-ass may need them. A startle can is an empty soda can with a few pennies, pebbles, or dried corn inside it, enough to make a loud rattle. Put the stones or pennies in the can and tape the opening shut with duct tape. A startle chain is a simple piece of linked metal chain about eighteen inches long and having no sharp protruding ends or edges.

Both tools are used, as their name implies, to startle your dog away from something she is doing. It is used only when you want her to run away from something—it will not bring her to you. Use it to stop negative or destructive behaviors in a dog that ignores your verbal "no." The first time you use either of these tools you must throw them so that they actually hit the dog. Aim for her side and not her face or legs. The can or chain are light weight and will do no harm. The combination of the sound and the sudden fright of being hit with the object stops the behavior in its tracks. After the first time all you need to do is to shake the can or chain or throw them near the dog and she will run from it. If you use a startle can or chain you will need to keep one on hand in every room for awhile. You must be able to grab the tool immediately and use it while the behavior is happening—never after it's over. Catch your dog in the act with a firm "no" and the sound of the chain or can. As soon as she stops the behavior praise her. If you are consistent you will not need it long.

I learned to use the startle can with Copper who came to me at about a year old. As he grew healthier he became more inventive as a teenage gangster. He was tall enough to reach the tops of tables and counters and take things, especially food. Copper actually took bread from out of the toaster. He grabbed food from my hand and especially liked to bump my elbow when I raised my arm to drink coffee. When the coffee spilled I could hear him laugh and he considered it his best trick. At that time I lived in a duplex house that had rooms off a long central hall. Copper liked to hide in doorways and pounce on me when I walked down the hall. He would grab me by the ankles to knock me over and then kiss me. When I'd ask him, "When are you going to stop this and grow up?" his reply was always, "Fat chance!"

It took only about a week to change Copper's ways with the startle can. I kept one on the kitchen counter in front of the toaster and he never took anything from the counter again. I kept one in view on the dining room table and if he made a move toward my food or coffee I shook it. Shaking it was all it took. For a while I carried a can around with me everywhere. If I saw him ready to pounce in the hallway I rattled it. His silliness stopped. Copper still has some strange ways and is an inveterate clown. I'm a lenient pack leader. When people come to visit he likes to rub his face in their hair if he can reach them or if they (or I) sit on the floor. He teases Kali by calling her a dog until she jumps him and they scuffle. He still insists that he's a "Great Intergalactic Be-ing" but Kali is "just a dog."

Kali is much more fierce and her behavior is more destructive. She came to me angry and abused and now six years later is settling down. As a teenager I gave her stuffed toys to rip up to manage her anger. The dogs have their own toy box. When I leave the house she takes pillows from the couch and rips them up, though never attempts to do this when I'm home. Cinde did this with a bed pillow once and the mess was awesome. The solution was the same for both dogs: they must be crated when alone. Your teenager will also need to remain crated when alone until she outgrows her brattiness. The age for this varies by breed and by individual. When you think she is ready start by giving her short periods free from the crate and extend them once you know that she'll behave.

Another frustration with Kali is her destruction of plants. She eats them off at the roots and pulls vines off the fences though I supplement her food with greens. She even tears the buds and flowers off the roses since the bushes are protected by their thorns. When I asked her why she does it, she said, "because I like them." I have a seventy-foot yard and grow an extensive flower essence garden (Essential Essences). I don't want to restrict the dogs' running space—they need the full yard for exercise—but I want to protect my plants that line the yard perimeters. The solution has been to never let her watch me garden, as she imitates me by pulling and digging plants up. I also fence each plant or group of plants with two-foot-high chicken wire. The wire protects the plants but also makes weeding and gardening more difficult. Instead of caging the dog in this case, I've caged my plants!

Kali also digs some very deep holes in the yard and does so always at night. She is possibly chasing the southern toads that come out at night and escape pursuit by digging in. Occasionally she eats one and we deal with diarrhea, vomiting, excessive thirst, and body odor for a week. When the holes start reaching three feet wide and several feet deep I fill them using dog feces from my daily clean up. It keeps her from going back to at least that hole. To prevent her from digging out of the yard under the fence I have placed bricks just under the ground surface all the way around the yard. Cyclone fence wire or chicken wire can also be used for this.

My girl has also made it a policy never to come when called, obedience training or no. After a lot of frustration with this one, I have done what probably is a training no-no but it works. Every time I call Kali I stand at the porch door with a can of biscuits and I rattle them. If she comes, she gets one and I praise her. If she doesn't, the can gets put away and I go out and get her. She comes more frequently now without the biscuit can and always, if sometimes slowly, with it. Remember that Kali came to me quite abused and is a number two on the dominance scale. My problems with her are unusual in a grown dog but probably typical of teenagers. It takes until about six years old for a Siberian Husky to grow up emotionally and we are finally almost there. These are a stubborn breed of very free spirits but gentle unless abuse ruins them.

Kali's most serious teenage criminality was biting me. She started doing this in defiance during obedience training. People suggested that I punish her more severely but I didn't want a showdown that I might not win; the dog was too dominant. A friend then suggested that I bite her back. "She doesn't know you have teeth," the woman said. "Show her your teeth the way another dog would." The next time Kali bit me I took her soft pink nose in my teeth and bit down until she squealed. I didn't break the skin. When my friend came back to visit Kali told her, "She bit me." "And why did she do that?" my friend asked amused. Kali's reply was, "Because she's a bully." She has never bitten me again. (Don't try this with your dog.)

Dusty's trick of going through mine and other people's purses and suitcases was controlled by keeping them out of her reach. She was also an escape artist that rushed the door and headed for the pizza shop a few blocks away. Vigilance was the only answer. Obedience training for the sit-stay helps door rushing. She was otherwise well-behaved. Tiger had a habit of hiding things. She kept little stashes of kibble, pennies, crystals, bookmarks with tassels, and an occasional tampon under furniture or behind drapes. Unless something I really needed was missing I let her do it. Somehow with two other dogs she managed to protect her stashes. Tiger was extremely intelligent. Her stashes included usually halves of dog biscuits. She would eat half and keep half for later. This dog had crystals of her own and knew which were hers. Most of my dogs have not shown much inter- est in crystals, though if I give one to Kali she drops it in her water bowl. Some personality quirks are just to be enjoyed.

Your canine juvenile delinquent will come up with her own crimes. Obedience training with firmness, compassion, and love is your best option. The behavior will stop eventually, usually by the time most dogs are a year and a half or two years old. It's worth the wait and the work. Keep your sense of humor through the teenage months and remember that you love your dog. This period of brattiness is the last long haul in puppy raising.

grownups at last

I t's been a long haul but your dog is fully grown now, both emotionally and physically. Maturity comes at different ages for different breeds. Large dogs seem to grow up later with a full adult coat and filled-out chest developing only at three or four years. Smaller breeds mature sooner. Most puppies lose their fuzzy short puppy coats just after a year old and grow undercoats and longer and more adult fur. Adult grooming and clipping that begins with the mature coat helps your dog to look like the breed you chose. Emotional maturity also varies from breed to breed, with some dogs responsible adults at a year and others seeming to take decades.

Young dogs of most breeds need lots of exercise and providing it rewards you with better behavior. A tired dog doesn't get into mischief. Too many people with good intentions take on dogs with high exercise requirements; a dog that needs exercise and doesn't get it becomes destructive. When the movie *101 Dalmatians* came out at Christmas, 1996 dalmatian show breeders and purebred dog fanciers cringed. They knew that lots of people would want dalmatian puppies and that lots of them would be unable or unwilling to deal with the breed's needs.

Dalmatians need a great deal of exercise but how many Americans are willing to be physically active? How many of the people who bought Christmas puppies for the kids researched the breed's needs first? Most casual pet guardians also do not know about or refuse to use a crate for training, the best insurance possible against destructive behavior. Sure enough, Florida newscasts of September, 1997 reported hundreds of dalmatians flooding the animal shelters. Too many of them will die there. Last Christmas's cute puppy is now a nine- to twelve-month-old teenager at the height of her misbehaving. The fate of these dogs is a tragedy, only one of many in this society where human and animal life is disposable.

Traveling with Your Dog

Your best bet to keep your dog happy, interested, and exercised is to take her with you wherever and whenever you can. You have worked at training her as a puppy and in formal obedience so you can do this. In a dog pack the members go everywhere together. In the family-pack when you leave, your dog will learn to accept it without noise or destroying things—use the crate until she does—but she will never like it. There are many places a trained dog can go with her person. Take her to parks, to the beach, to street fairs, and to visit other people and animals.

Directories are available for traveling with your dog, and a pet that comes with her crate is usually welcome in motels and hotels. The AAA offers lodging information that includes whether pets may stay. A motel in Treasure Island, Florida, called The Lorelei is owned and run by a dog groomer, who makes animals welcome. Every room is equipped with food and water bowls and there is a swimming pool just for dogs. Each floor of the motel has gates at the stairways to keep dogs in their own neighborhood. Dog grooming and bathing are available and one floor is just for cats. The motel costs no more than other motels in this tourist beach area. The Valley Forge motel nearby in St. Petersburg has a sign on its marquee reading "Pets Welcome." These are vacation places to matronize.

If you plan to travel make reservations in advance for you and your dog. Call ahead and make sure pets are welcome. Some motel chains allow pets and others do not. If you live in a hurricane or other disaster-prone area, as I do in Florida, you will want to know which motels you may go to in an emergency. Hurricane shelters do not accept pets and I cannot consider them an option. In case of evacuation the dogs and I go together. I will not be separated from them. During the 1992 Hurricane Andrew, many homes were destroyed and thousands of dogs and cats were set free. Many people never saw their pets again. The same situation happens in earthquakes when there is no warning or time to prepare. The people of Monserrat Island face this difficulty with the volcano eruptions.

What to Do When Your Dog Can't Travel with You

For times when you can't take your dog along you will have to consider a boarding kennel or a house sitter. Leaving your dog alone in the yard with a neighbor's child to feed her once a day is not an option. It is frightening and upsetting to a dog who feels abandoned, and your neighbors will not thank you for her howling. Because of her anxiety and fear that you may not return, she may become destructive. The child may forget to feed her or give her water. This is absolutely unfair to your dog. You may also have negative experiences with allowing a friend or acquaintance to stay in your home while you are away. I have had two very bad experiences doing so and will not repeat them. The person who seems to get along so well with your dog may not get along when you are away. Your dog will become anxious even if she knows the sitter and will likely misbehave. The person may be less reliable than you expect or even less honest. Don't allow your dog to suffer.

There are two better options. One is a professional pet sitter that makes her living taking care of other people's animals. She will come to meet your dogs before you travel and will ask you detailed questions about their habits and needs. She will walk and feed them at the times they are used to, give supplements or medications, play with them, and exercise them until they are tired. She will also take in your mail, water houseplants, turn lights on and off, and make sure your home is secure. Many of these people are veterinary technicians or simply very experienced in handling dogs. Your dog groomer, obedience school, or holistic veterinarian can recommend a qualified pet sitter or you can find one by word of mouth. Interview the person and watch her interaction with your dog. Ask for references. In some states pet sitters must be licensed. You will know when you return—by your pet's physical and emotional state and behavior and the condition of your home—if the sitter is the right one to use again.

Your other option is a boarding kennel. A good one may not be easy to locate and most areas offer few choices. Some veterinarians board dogs but be sure that your healthy dogs are not housed with sick ones. Veterinarians may also lack the space for housing large dogs—you don't want yours left in a cage for a week. Look for adequate runs wherever you board. If you have more than one dog and they get along well you will want them kept together in as large a pen or run as possible. Most boarding kennels and veterinarians do not walk the dogs outside, though some have indoor-outdoor runs. Indoors-only can create problems with a puppy still in house-training; you may have to start the training process all over again when you come home. When cats are boarded at a mixed-pet kennel they should have a room separate from the dogs.

If you use alternative vaccinations you may also have difficulty with your boarding kennels. Most kennels require the standard vaccinations including rabies and bordatella yearly. Some will accept your signing a release form. Some will accept your holistic veterinarian's letter stating that your dog is fully protected. Some will not, however. The kennel may be willing to feed your preservative-free food if you provide it. They will usually give your dog a bath at the end of the stay and may require it. You can usually request that chemical flea shampoos not be used. Kennels generally disinfect dog runs with strong cleaners mixed with or followed by bleach. The bleach can cause burn marks on the feet of sensitive dogs. Some kennels will respect your wishes to protect your dog from this but others will not. I stopped using one veterinary boarding kennel because of the burns on Copper's feet and legs that the standard vet refused to take responsibility for.

Before leaving your dog at any kennel go and see it. Is it clean? How big are the runs? Avoid unclean kennels or those where your dog is kept twenty-four hours a day in a cage. Is there indoor-outdoor space? This is ideal in moderate climates, but may not be so in the south. Is the kennel air-conditioned in hot climates, or heated in very cold ones? Are the dogs walked or left in their pens to eliminate? Adult dogs adjust to not being walked more easily than puppies do.

What are the animals fed and can you bring your own preservative-free food? Is there space for all the dogs of a family to room together? Kali and Copper get the "family room," a pen about twelve feet square, where I board them; they are also walked. What are the bathing requirements? It is best if your dog has a bath at the end of her stay to prevent her bringing home fleas. Some kennels require it and you will have to pay extra for it.

The cost of pet sitting is per visit and if you want your dog walked four times a day you will pay more than if the sitter comes only three times. Your adult dog should be visited a minimum of three times. More is better; puppies more frequently yet. Boarding kennels cost by the day and prices are based on the size and weight of the dog. There is usually a discount if you board more than one pet together. Baths cost extra and are also based on weight. Some kennels offer full grooming services. Kali and Copper could probably stay at the nearest Hilton for what it costs when I board them. They are happy with the kennel they go to, however, and I know they are safe there. When I'm away and have to leave them I feel confident of the care and treatment they receive.

When you come home and bring your dogs home, notice their appearance and watch your dog's behavior. If she looks and smells good, has not lost or gained much weight, and does not bring home fleas you probably have a good kennel. Watch her behavior. Does the dog seem excited to be home or cowed and upset from the experience? Excitement is normal, upset dogs are not. My dogs come home happy but very tired. It may take a few times before your dog accepts being boarded. She may have tantrums when she sees a suitcase. This is normal. I have to pack mine inside a cupboard when Kali is outside and take the suitcase out only when it's time to actually leave. When she comes home, she's happy, however. Copper, on the other hand, is delighted with his vacation. Avoid long good-byes when leaving your pet at a kennel or with a sitter. Anxiety on your part will only trigger your dog's separation worries.

You will need to make reservations with a pet sitter or kennel as far in advance as possible. Good kennels fill up and good pet sitters stay busy. If you wish to travel over a holiday it is especially important to make early reservations.

Some kennels have only a few large runs and you must make specific reservations for them. Pet sitters can visit only so many houses a day. Once you find a good kennel or sitter, stay with them; they will become familiar and safe for your dog. It may take a few tries to find the one your animals can be happy with and you feel confident with. If you have any doubts about your dog's treatment or safety, seek another place. Remember that whenever you can take your dog with you, she will be happier.

Adding a New Pet to Your Family

As your dog grows out of puppyhood and teenage delinquency you may decide to add another pet to your family. Two animals together keep each other company and are no more work than having one. If you have socialized your dog to other animals as a puppy and if she is not aggressive the additional animal should be easy. Beware, however, of adopting animals that your dog may perceive as prey. You would be horrified if your dog killed—or worse killed and ate—a bird, rabbit, or gerbil, though she would only be following instinct to do so. Such small pets must be kept far out of reach and this may not be possible in your home. If your dog has been raised from puppyhood with a bird or rodent, you may have raised her to accept these pets. She may respect the bird or gerbil she knows, but attack a strange one of the same species. A very small dog may be less a threat to these caged animals.

Cinde considered any small animal to be a puppy and her response was to try and nurse it. She tried this with a pair of rabbits, several cats, and any number of small dogs. The cats and rabbits responded easily to her kindness, but the tiny dogs were offended. Even when they snapped at her, she continued mothering them. She once followed a turtle around a friend's kitchen totally mystified, but didn't try to harm it. She never threatened or harmed any creature of any type and raised Tiger and Tiger's puppies as if they were her own. I could have brought any animal into the house with Cinde there. Not only would she have protected it, but she would have trained the puppies in her care to protect it also, as she trained Tiger to worship cats and small animals, too.

Many families raise dogs and cats together. The best way to do this is from the beginning when your dog is a puppy. Dogs raised with cats learn to respect them fully. If you have socialized your dog to cats as a puppy she is unlikely to be a threat to them, even if a cat has not lived with you yet. When you bring a cat into your house for the first time, let your dog sniff the cat carrier and examine the protected cat. If you can do this on neutral ground, not in your home, (that is, not in your dog's territory), so much the better. You may have to keep the cat crated for a day or so and certainly separate them overnight when you can't watch the dog. When you feel that the dog will accept the cat, let her out of the carrier but put your dog on leash at first.

Let the cat explore your home freely for a few minutes while keeping your dog from chasing her. Give an obedience correction and a firm "no" if the dog lunges at the cat. Once the cat and dog know each other and you feel the dog is not a threat, let your dog free but leave her leash on and dragging at first. Keep their time together short and then separate them until they know each other and have made friends. When you cannot be there to supervise keep the animals separated, especially when you leave the house, until you are completely sure of their behavior together.

Each pet in the family should have her own sleeping place and own food and water bowls. Place cat bowls and litter boxes up high where dogs can't reach them. Dogs like cat food because of its higher protein. They like cat stool for the same reason and eating stool can spread parasites. Keep the cat from entering the dog's crate, her private space and sanctuary, and from unduly teasing the dog. It is probably best to adopt a cat with claws so she will have some protective defense. Declawing is inhumane—without claws the cat is helpless. With just a few sharp paw swipes your cat will teach the dog to respect her. Expect a lot of hissing, clawing, and chasing at first; most of it will stop. Cats consider dogs an inferior species.

Soon after I got Copper I boarded him and Dusty with a dog groomer friend. I had no idea of his temperament around animals other than dogs at that time. The groomer took both dogs home with her at night. She had other dogs and a cat. She closed my dogs into separate rooms and left them there. The next morning she opened the door to find Copper and her cat together. She had not known the cat was there. Copper had a large scratch on his nose but he was curled up with the cat asleep when she opened the door. They were best of friends after that. Unfortunately, the friendship (or armed truce) held only for that particular cat. Copper informed me one year that he wanted "Socks for Christmas." "What would a dog do with Socks?" I wanted to know. "Eat it," he replied with a sneer, showing me a picture of a gray neighborhood cat with white feet. Santa didn't fill his stocking.

Bringing a second dog home when your first dog is socialized is easier. Try to introduce them on neutral territory, letting them make friends before bringing the newcomer into your yard or house. Keep your first dog on a leash and let the new dog explore, or you may put the new dog in her own crate while they sniff at each other. The new dog needs her own crate, sleeping place, collar and leash, bowls, and toys. Your first dog may not forgive it if you put the new pup in her crate or offer the new dog her belongings. Dogs are territorial and can be jealous, and she will take her jealousy out on the newcomer, not on you. Supervise their interactions at first and separate them when you can't watch them. Your current dog's typical response will be to snub the new pet but she'll warm up in time, much quicker than a cat will warm up to a dog.

Whether the newcomer is a dog or cat, make sure your current dog gets the lion's share of attention for a while. The newcomer will not expect it and probably needs some space to get used to things anyhow. If you think your dog could be a threat to a cat, it would be best to adopt another dog instead. Few dogs will injure a puppy. If your newcomer is grown, a dog of the opposite sex usually is more likely to be accepted than one of the same sex. A neutered male dog is less likely to fight another male, neutered or not. A male dog is unlikely to harm a female dog but females can be aggressive toward males. Your dogs will work out a pack order together and some scuffling and snapping may happen along the way. Let them work it out as long as no one's getting hurt. Send them to their crates for time out or separate them in another way if they get too rough or rowdy. Two dogs will chase each other and play together and eventually a cat and dog may play together, too. It's wonderful to watch.

I recently asked Copper if we could bring a new dog home. His response was to ask me, "Is there enough food?" When I assured him there was he agreed. He asked for another boy. When I asked Kali, she was less pleased. "Only if I'm the best," she said. Siberian Huskies are close enough to their wolf ancestors to be good pack animals and they have more invested in dog social interactions than in those with people. I find that all of my dogs have been happier in pairs than alone, but that three can be too much to handle. I would not consider a cat, however, or other small animal as I doubt I could keep it safe. Both Copper and Kali have caught small animals in the yard; Copper has killed birds and Kali fruit rats. Copper was tremendously proud of himself with his kill and ate it to the last feather. Kali was upset about the rat and when I asked her why, she replied, "It didn't stay to play with me."

Remember that your expenses increase with a second pet. You will spend more in food and supplies, veterinary bills, and boarding for two than for one. Both pets require your attention and playtime, though two animals will also play with each other. An older dog with a young puppy or cat will exercise more and may get a new lease on life. The older dog needs private space where she can withdraw from the newcomer, too. The younger dog needs training and a puppy needs house-training. Can you handle the mess or the time these take just when your first dog's care becomes easy? Many families are two-dog or dog-and-cat families and feel it is worth the work. I personally prefer more than one dog at a time though the stress of introducing a newcomer can be high for awhile.

Teaching Your Dog Tricks and Games

As your dog becomes older and more stable you may wish to teach her some tricks and games. These don't degrade her dignity but enhance her sense of showmanship. When your dog wants something she will sometimes paw you. Use that action to teach her to shake by taking her paw and praising her while saying, "shake" or "paw." Once she knows "shake," ask her to do so, praise her, put her leg down, then say "other paw," and pick up her other foreleg. Praise her again. She will get the idea quickly. You may use food treats more often when teaching tricks than when obedience training. After all, it's a game.

Watch your dog to see what she likes to do and then turn it into a trick. Kali has always brought me her stuffed toys to throw. When I threw them sometimes she brought them back and other times she didn't. When she'd bring me toys I began to take them from her saying "give it to me" and saying "get it" when I threw it. She quickly learned to retrieve the toys for me to throw again. If your dog barks at a particular time, tell her to "speak" when she is doing so anyway. Eventually she will associate the word with the action and speak on command. If she barks repeatedly let her do it once or twice then say "enough" and make her stop. This is also a good way to deal with a dog that barks too much. Teach her to bark on command—and to stop on command. Praise her immediately when she does what you ask.

Repetition is the key to teaching anything. You may use food treats to bait the dog into the action you desire from her. Get her to roll over by holding a biscuit close to her nose when she is lying down. She will follow the biscuit into the action. As soon as she does what you wanted her to do, give the action a name, give her the treat, and praise her. Dogs are no dummies; they learn quickly. If your dog runs for her leash at walk time it's only another step to have her bring her leash to you. Dogs will also carry things and large dogs can be taught to wear a saddlebag-type backpack. There are many books on teaching dogs tricks.

There is no need to limit your vocabulary of commands to standard obedience. Your dog understands more than you can imagine and a little teaching or just talking go a long way. Use the same words for each action and talk conversationally to your dog. My dogs understand "go to bed," "go to your crate," "go lie down," "in the house," "let's go out," "enough," "off," and "walk." They understand much more and know when I'm going out and where I'm going. If I say "dog dinners" they both go on red alert. "Bedtime" means the dogs go outside one last time for the night, and "in the house" means it's time to go indoors. Our pets are not dumb animals; they understand everything we say and are aware of everything that happens in their environment.

As your dog grows older, your ability to communicate psychically with her improves. Your adult dog has a lot more to say than a puppy does and a longer attention span for both training and communicating. This is the time when you begin to have interesting discussions with your dog. Where a puppy might only giggle at you, your grown dog can hold a conversation. When teaching her something try showing her a picture of what you want her to do while speaking the command word you've chosen. If there are problems like digging or barking too much you may be able to solve them by psychic communication. Ask her why she is doing the thing you want her to stop and if she will please stop doing it. You may have to understand her reasoning first or give her something else she wants.

How to Ease the Trauma of Moving to a New Home

One instance when communication is crucial is if you are planning to move. A dog will become terrified at the packing and activity. Any change in her environment or routine is threatening and now her home is disappearing into boxes and your stress and anxiety are evident. It is extremely important to reassure your animals frequently that "it's okay, we're all going together." Try to show them pictures of the new place, especially their new yard, and how you will all get there. Tell them again and again, "We're going together and you'll like it."

This reassurance is especially necessary for a dog that has come from a shelter. Moving in the past may have meant she went to the pound, the most stressful and dangerous place of all. If so, your moving may make her fear that the end of her life with you is near, or the end of her life, period. A dog that has never seen moving time may be equally anxious, fearing the unknown instead of the awful known. A dog that has moved a few times with you will be stressed, but less afraid. Moving is an instance when your dog needs your help and psychic communication can be a way to give it. Use flower essences to help during this stressful time, starting a month before and continuing until a month after the move. Try Bach's Walnut and Rescue Remedy/Calming Essence or Essential Essence's Comfort Essence or Pet Rescue Combination.

As the time draws closer to the move, during the van loading, and for several weeks after the move to the new home be very careful that your dog doesn't get loose. She may run in panic into traffic or try to find her old neighborhood. She may not know how to return to you. Make sure her identification tags are up to date. Notify the tattoo or microchip registration center and local dog license office of your new address and phone number. If you must travel long distance with your dog by ground or air make sure the tags for your new address and phone number are always on your dog. By this time your dog is a part of your family and you don't want to lose her.

As your dog gets older she will have different needs than she did as a puppy or young adult. The next chapter discusses the aging dog.

old age and dying

Puppies grow so fast. Before you know it they are grown and suddenly they are old. It seems so unfair that dogs don't stay with us through our lifetimes. They come and go so quickly, no matter how fiercely we love them, and they leave a terrible void in our lives when they are gone. Few dogs today live beyond ten or twelve years. Large and giant breeds have a lower life span than small dogs. Placing your dog on a holistic diet and using the least toxic route for immunizations and medical treatment will go far toward extending your pet's life. It will also raise her quality of life for as long as she lives. Good training and socialization helps your dog to live longer, too. A well-trained dog lives under less stress and her good behavior keeps her welcome in her home. Investing in a securely fenced yard will also help to protect your pet. Remember to have an identifying microchip inserted or keep a current identification tag on at all times.

An older dog is a joy to live with. She knows you as thoroughly as you know her and your habits fit together perfectly. Her teenage wildness and shenanigans are past, her strenuous obedience training is over, and she is cooperative and loving. She isn't trying anymore to be leader of the pack, but is willing to sit back and let you do it. If younger animals have joined the family she has had a hand in their training and you and they benefit tremendously. An old dog teaches the new one the ropes and makes sure the newcomer behaves. It's a wonderful process to watch. Your old dog will look long into your eyes and commune lovingly with you. Such eye searching sessions are beautiful and tender. Learn psychic communication and talk to your pet at this time of her life. Her wisdom and perspective on every aspect of living will astound you.

Not even your best care can prevent your dog from aging, but holistic care and treatment make it easier and more comfortable. Allopathic medications and interventions leave a dog or human miserable because of side effects; holistic treatments do not. More and more dogs are on long-term allopathic medicines for chronic dis-eases that develop much less frequently in holistically raised pets. If the medication stops a symptom it creates another one. Chemical drugs shorten lives. I have witnessed too many dog guardians resort to euthanasia rather than let their pets suffer from standard veterinary practice. If the treatment is worse than the dis-ease, something is terribly wrong. Your aging pet's best friends are natural remedies and a holistic veterinarian. Dis-eases that the standard veterinary system has no answers for can respond readily to simple holistic treatments.

Your older dog needs an easier life than the one she led when she was in her prime. If you are used to jogging with your dog you may need to switch to walking or decreasing the distance. Jogging is hard on aging joints and hearts. If she enjoys playing frisbee be careful to throw it no higher than shoulder height. Your dog may prefer jumping for the disc but it puts her at risk for spinal injuries (this is true for dogs of all ages). As your dog slows down, be aware of her fatigue and don't push her beyond her endurance. Though she will try to do everything she had in the past, she may not be strong enough now.

Your dog will need more protection from extremes of cold and heat and a softer place to sleep. If she is used to sleeping on your bed she may have difficulty climbing there. Place a stool or bench at the foot to give her a step up or build a ramp. Don't exile her if she has slept there all her life. Your dog may need a boost to help her in and out of your car as well.

Schedules may become increasingly important. She wants her dinner on time and her walks when they are "supposed" to happen. Her elimination will be more dependable if she keeps to her schedule, reducing constipation and incontinence problems. An incontinent dog can be treated by adding wheat germ oil or essential fatty acids (flax seed oil) to her food and by acupuncture and homeopathy. Constipation may be aided by digestive enzymes and a few more vegetables and fruit in her diet. An older dog sleeps more and should have an undisturbed place to do so. Her crate by now has become her doghouse. Place a soft pad or pillow in it and leave the door open. Keep her private space off limits to children and other pets and honor her need for privacy when she enters her crate. If she has become cranky in her old age, teach children to respect her.

Common Maladies with an Older Dog

An old dog may become overweight or underweight, suffer tooth decay and bad breath, constipation, warts and tumors, thinning coats, arthritis, declining sight and hearing, and organ and mental failures. If your dog has been on an optimal diet many of these symptoms can be minimized. Warts and tumors are direct vaccinosis symptoms. Arthritis may arise from many years of vitamin C and mineral deficiencies. Some organ and sensory failures can be prevented by lifelong quality diets while others are simply due to aging. If you have routinely cleaned your dog's teeth or had your veterinarian do it, you will have fewer problems with the dog's mouth. Infected teeth and gums create a systemic bacterial problem that can shorten your dog's life. If her mouth hurts, it will also effect her eating and chewing.

It is never too late to start putting your dog on a natural diet. An older dog may not like to give up the same old stuff she's been eating for ten years but you can mix the old food with the new for a while. Gradually increase the preservative-free food and reduce the supermarket junk. As with a puppy, grate the vegetables you put in her food, starting with small amounts and increasing gradually to prevent diarrhea. If her teeth hurt, you may wish to soften her food by mixing kibble with warm water or soup broth. If your dog has been on a less than optimal diet for long the natural diet may promote an intestinal house-cleaning. This means that about a week after starting the better food she may develop diarrhea, increased urination, and body odor. The detoxification is not a sign of dis-ease but of healing. It generally lasts a week or two. Let the process of the toxins leaving her body continue. When shedding time comes she may shed her fur more thoroughly than usual. The new coat that comes in will show you clearly the benefits of the new food.

An old dog can go through at least partial vaccinosis antidoting, but leave this to your holistic veterinarian. She will probably wish to treat your dog constitutionally, which means a treatment that takes the whole dog and all her needs into account along with her vaccination record. Clearing your dog's years of vaccination side-effects can be the answer to many dis-eases but too extensive detoxification in old age is probably to be avoided. Warts and tumors are vaccinosis symptoms that can disappear with antidoting and every organ of the dog's body is renewed. If your dog's skin develops warts be careful not to make them bleed when brushing or clipping her. Your dog groomer is already aware of this tendency in aging dogs. Some breeds are more prone to warts than others and cocker spaniels routinely develop them. Boxers are a breed prone to tumors. *Thuja* is the vaccinosis antidote for warts, tumors, and growths of all kinds.

A woman whose older miniature poodle was experiencing heart dis-ease and high blood pressure once called me. She was distressed by the allopathic treatment of her current vet and by the vet's pessimism. Her dog slept all the time on the medications, but otherwise seemed no stronger. When I found her a holistic veterinarian in her area and she changed her pet's diet the difference was almost immediate. The veterinarian placed the dog on vitamins C and E, spirulina, and hawthorn berry herb syrup. The dog is still alive years later and at seventeen years of age she looks healthier and happier. Her person says she looks and acts like a young dog. I have seen many instances where homeopathy and natural healing can give new life to old pets.

Arthritis is another problem for many aging animals especially large breed dogs. There is a tendency in large breeds for chronic vitamin C deficiencies that manifest as a form of subclinical scurvy. The dog will experience gum dis-ease and loose teeth along with stiff and painful joints. This is the reason for vitamin C supplementation during all phases of a dog's lifetime. Unlike humans, dogs produce vitamin C in their bodies but the amounts they can produce are not enough for today's polluted and toxic environments and high stress. The vitamin detoxifies the body of these contaminants but is also depleted by them. An arthritic dog can be much helped by adding some supplements to her diet. Vitamins C and E are highly important (see the chapter on Nutrition). Glucosamine and chondroitin or an enzyme called SOD (superoxide dismutase) can be the answer to arthritis pain and joint inflammation. Other remedies include Glycoflex—a marine mussel—shark cartilage, or beef cartilage (simple gelatin capsules). Determine the proper dose by body weight and mix these health food store supplements into your dog's food.

Mental problems in elderly dogs can be alleviated with vitamins C and B-complex—they heal the blood vessels and increase circulation—and with an herb called ginkgo biloba that is being used for humans with Alzheimer's disease. Gentle detoxification will also be important but if your dog is frail go carefully with this. HomeoVetix offers a variety of homeopathic combinations for pet detoxification and Newton's Pet Detoxifier is excellent. Grate a small amount of raw carrots or beets (half teaspoonful to start) into food as a detoxifier. Beets in food make the dog's urine red but the reaction is safe. Liquid chlorophyll may also be added to food to oxygenate the blood and additionally is an aid to body odor.

If your dog's body has odor she needs detoxification. Watch her eliminations to make sure she is not constipated. Digestive enzymes are a good suggestion for all aging dogs. Older dogs may experience increased frequency of anal impaction and this needs to be watched and taken care of. An optimal diet is your best bet for overweight or underweight dogs. If she is overweight, remember that she is less active and may need less food. Some older dogs require a lower level of protein in their diet. Preservative-free formulas that are lower in protein are readily available for senior dogs. Detoxification may also help a dog whose senses are failing. These dogs are less able to take care of themselves and need more supervision and protection from accidents and harm, especially when outdoors.

Your pet's emotional state is also a factor in her quality and length of life. Many an old dog has decided not to go on if her person dies before her or if she loses the home she has lived in all her life. A dog that feels she has been replaced by a younger animal and is no longer wanted will also die sooner than she may have otherwise. Keep your dog feeling secure, needed, and loved. A dog that loses a beloved pet or human friend grieves as much as any grieving human and can become depressed. Prozac is not the answer—I am appalled at the current allopathic trend of giving animals psychotropic drugs—but love and consideration are. Give your dog lots of special times with you, lots of petting, gentle walks and visits, cuddling and play times. Talk to her frequently, verbally and psychically, keep the stress in her life as low as possible, and let her know how much you love her and need her.

Coping with Your Dog's Death

Despite all your best care, the end eventually comes. You may have to make the wrenching decision to euthanize her, or your dog may die suddenly. Neither way is ever easy. Some dogs have been known to seek their own deaths, running off uncharacteristically to be killed by automobiles or simply to disappear into the woods when they feel their time has come. A dog at her time to die will hold on as long as possible if you ask her to but this may not be in her best interest if she is suffering. An animal in pain or misery whose prognosis can only be further degeneration until death is best not permitted more suffering. As hard as the decision is to euthanize your dog, it may be more humane.

Use psychic communication to find out what your dog wants and needs. Tell her you love her deeply and will miss her forever when she goes but that you respect her wishes. Ask her if she wants to be put down or to tell you when that time comes. You will hear and understand her responses clearly as her participation is important to her. Dogs trade in their outworn bodies readily—they do not have the fear of death that humans have. They know they reincarnate and will return. When her body becomes uninhabitable, your dog will readily release it. She'll come back in a new body and often will return to you.

Cinde died at nine years old of breast cancer. I put her through surgery though I already suspected that her dis-ease was not an abscess, but was terminal. A female dog who has not been spayed before her first heat is susceptible to this dis-ease. If your dog has been used for breeding, but is now finished having litters, spay her. Even if she is past middle age, talk to your veterinarian about the advisability of the surgery. Cinde survived her cancer surgery by only a few weeks. It became clear that she was not recovering and was suffering. I had her euthanized.

Tiger also died of cancer and like Cinde did it in a way I will never accept again. She simply stopped eating and starved herself to death. I knew that she was dying and so did my veterinarian. The vet felt that she was not suffering and that I would know when the time came to euthanize her. Over a period of three months she grew thinner and thinner despite all I could tempt her with. She had talked to me nonstop since I brought her home when she was five weeks old, but, she refused to talk to me. She told me every time I tried, "Go away, I'm not here now." I never thought to ask her if she wanted me to put her down; I was holding onto her too tightly. She became so weak that I had to carry her outside to eliminate but she never once eliminated indoors. I lifted her onto my bed every night; she had always slept with me and now was too weak to climb on the bed herself. One night she put her head in my lap and I clearly heard her say, "I love you but I have to go now." The next morning she was unconscious and I took her to be euthanized.

Perhaps I learn slowly, but I learn. When Tiger's daughter Dusty died it was of cancer again, this time of the lungs. My vet had warned me a year earlier that there was a mass in her lungs and now Dusty's breathing was becoming more and more labored. She woke me repeatedly at night with panic attacks, either from lack of oxygen or senility (which can also be from lack of oxygen or from the cancer itself). "She's playing the same tape over again and again," my vet said. As the summer got hotter she seemed more in distress. Finally one night I hugged and petted her and asked her, "Dusty, do you want to go?" "Yes," the dog replied. "Do you want me to take you to the vet to die?" I asked her again to make sure she understood. "Yes," she repeated, "I want to go." "When do you want me to do it?" I asked her. "Tomorrow," she said. When I took her to be euthanized she quickly led me into the veterinarian's office, showing more vitality than she had in a long time.

After it was over that night, she came to me while I meditated. I saw her running happily through a field of flowers. "Don't worry," she said. "I'll be back." Though I often saw Tiger in my meditations and rituals for the first years after her death, Dusty did not come to me in that way. When Kali came out of her airline box I was totally surprised at how much she resembled Dusty in appearance and energy. I finally asked Kali, "Are you Dusty?" and she said yes. Perhaps because I was living in a new place by this time, Kali was convinced that the past life was mine and not hers when she had last been with me. She picked up her competition and rivalry with Copper immediately. "Do you remember Copper," I asked her. "Oh Him!" she said, "I know him all right." Copper recognized her, too.

Dogs have souls and souls reincarnate. We do not end with one lifetime but have been on Earth in a variety of bodies many many times. Dogs can reincarnate interchangeably as cats and horses, too, and as other animals. I was riding in a car once when I witnessed another car strike a stocky medium-sized black dog. I got out to help. The dog was dying, the blood coming from her mouth indicated internal injuries, and I sat with her at the side of the street and stroked and talked to her as she died. She had a story. She had been a bear in most of her other lives and was very afraid of people. For this incarnation it was decided that she come in a form that would put her closer to people so she could learn to be less afraid. Unfortunately, she had been quite neglected by the people she came to live with. She ran the streets and they forgot to feed her. She missed being a bear, didn't like the city noise and smells, had itchy, sore skin, and she wanted to leave. She stepped in front of the car deliberately, so that the driver couldn't avoid hitting her. She was going home to be a bear again by her own choice.

I once asked Copper why he didn't want his toenails cut. He showed me himself as a red roan horse that was being shod. He hated the shoeing and may have been abused in the process. In that lifetime he fought having his feet trimmed as he does in this one. "Two wrongs don't make a right," I told him. "That's right," he said, "don't touch my feet." I asked him if he had been a dog in other lifetimes, too. "Sure," he said. "What kind of dog were you?" I asked him. "A nice one," said Copper. He wouldn't tell me more about it. I am sure that when Copper dies he will return to me quickly.

For years after Tiger died she came to me in dreams. Every year at Hallows, the Wiccan New Year and honoring of the dead, Tiger would enter whatever ritual or meditation I did. Once a little girl saw her in the circle and often adults did. She came for the length of the ritual and left when the circle was opened. After ten years I still have hopes of her returning.

If your dog has died, you may contact her in meditation the same way you spoke psychically with her alive. You may or may not be able to reach her; if she has just died try that night then let her rest for at least a few weeks or a month before trying again. When the time comes to bring a new puppy home, something best not done immediately after your old dog's death, meditate and ask to contact your dog that died. Ask her if she would like to come back to you with the new puppy. If she agrees, ask her to show you what she will look like in her new incarnation and how you will find her.

After you bring your new puppy home, pick a time when the puppy is asleep, put your hands gently on her and go into meditation. Ask to speak to your old dog. Ask her if she can accept the puppy you are holding as her new body. If she agrees invite her to come into the puppy. If done before ten weeks of age, your puppy's spirit has not fully entered her body. Her personality is not yet established and your old dog may enter if you and she choose. Later this will not work. If you bring home an older dog, however, you may be aware that she resembles or has the same personality traits of your old dog. Psychically ask her if she is that dog. You may be surprised. Kali told me that she had been Dusty and was supposed to find me.

The dog that is a reincarnation of a former pet will not act just like her and may not physically look like her. You will nevertheless be aware of an unmistakably familiar energy. Kali does not like to be compared with Dusty and Dusty was definitely more mellow. Resemblances creep through frequently enough to know that they are the same spirit but your new pet must be allowed to be herself. It is probably best to wait some time between your old dog's death and bringing home a new dog for several reasons. First, to allow your own grieving process to be completed unimpeded. Second, to keep you from comparing your new dog's every action with the old one's, whether she is a reincarnation or not. Third, to give your dog a chance to recover and heal on the other side before asking her to come back. Dusty died two years to the week before Kali came to me as an six- to eight-month-old puppy.

Remember that every dog you live with and love has her own personality and spirit. And every dog's personality and spirit is one to love. Even if the old dog you loved so deeply is gone, your new dog needs and deserves your love. She may or may not be a dog you loved before but she is there to be loved fully now. Do not add another pet to your life until you are ready to love the new dog fully, whether she may be a reincarnation of the dog you lost or not. To do otherwise is unfair to your new pet. If she is a reincarnation, you may find that she was with you long ago and is not the dog that most recently died. Welcome and love her whoever she may be. She has come to you for a reason.

Dogs as well as people have karma and your karma is to be together. Karma is the law of returning actions and reincarnation is the law of returning spirits. A dog's life purpose is the job that she has in being with you. Perhaps that job is to teach you to be a responsible pet guardian. Perhaps it is to teach you to love unconditionally or it is her job to protect and take care of you. Whatever the job, you and your dog have been brought together for it, to live together and love each other and explore the nature of your togetherness and lives. Honor your pet for the job she does for you. Do your part of the bargain by giving her the most love and the best life that you can for every moment she is with you. When your dog dies, honor her for her many gifts and also know that you have done your best for her. No matter what you have done or not done, know that she loves you totally, maybe more than any other living Be-ing could ever love.

Life comes around and goes around. Your old dog has died and you are about to start a new life with a new puppy. When something ends something else always is ready to begin. A new life is ready to enter your guardianship and care. I wish you good luck and much love with your new puppy.

Full Moon in Pisces
September 16, 1997

some commonly used homeopathic remedies

Aconitum napellus—First onset of any dis-ease, fright, accidents and injuries, burns, fear of thunder.

Apis mellifica—Bee or other insect stings, fire ant bites, sudden swelling and redness, ear or eye inflammation, raw eczema.

Arnica montana—Injuries, bruises, trauma, any accident, after surgeries, after seizures or bone fractions, strains, after giving birth. Arnica salves are used only when the skin is unbroken.

Arsenicum album—Itching, hot spots, skin sores and eczema, acute vomiting and diarrhea, gastritis, parvovirus; the animal shows extreme restlessness.

Belladonna—Hot conditions, sudden and violent onset of fever and heat, redness, inflammations, heat stroke. The skin seems to radiate heat and the pet is dull and unresponsive.

Bryonia alba—For all conditions that become worse with movement, arthritis, bordatella/kennel cough, nosebleeds.

Carbo veg—Gas and constipation, collapse and shock.

Chamomilla—Most dis-eases that occur during teething, primary puppy remedy, cranky, wants to be held.

Cina—Roundworms in puppies.

Cocculus—Motion sickness, car sickness.

Felix mas—Tapeworms.

Gelsemium—Shyness, fear and fright, sneezing, upper respiratory distemper-type symptoms.

Hepar sulph—Infections with pus discharge, infected ears, boils, abscesses, dermatitis with discharge.

Hypericum—Pain after bruising and accidents, nerve pain, nervous conditions, irritability and hyperactivity, seizures, stress reliever, immunity builder.

Ipecac—Repeated vomiting.

Mercurius cor—Dysentery, parvovirus, diarrhea, wet eczema.

Natrum muriaticum—Bad attitude, adolescent dogs, good for shelter rescues' past abuse, grieving dogs, dogs that are standoffish and want to be left alone especially when ill, dogs that startle easily at sudden or loud noises.

Nux vomica—Gastritis from garbage can raiding or over-eating.

Podophyllum—Puppy diarrhea, use with *Chamomilla*.

Pulsatilla—Clinging whiny puppies, separation anxiety, usually puppies of light coloring.

Rhus tox—Any condition that eases after warm-up movement, fevers, arthritis, sprains, rashes, poison ivy.

Scutellaria—Training problems, behavior problems, adolescent misbehavior, seizures.

Silica—Chronic problems and infections of all sorts, recurrent dis-eases, hot spots.

Sulfur—Vaccinosis antidote when dog has dry eczema, chronic dermatitis, mange, dandruff, chronic diarrhea, fever, rheumatism or incontinence.

Thuja—Primary vaccinosis antidote, for tumors, warts, and growths.

Urtica urens—Burns, scalds, rashes, fevers.

bibliography

Gwen Bailey. *The Perfect Puppy: How to Raise a Well-Behaved Dog*. Pleasantville, NY, Reader's Digest, 1995.

Wendell O. Belfield, DVM and Martin Zucker. *How to Have A Healthier Dog: The Benefits of Vitamins and Minerals for Your Dog's Life Cycles*. New York, NY, New American Library, 1981.

Carol Lea Benjamin. *Second Hand Dog: How to Turn Yours into a First Rate Pet*. New York, Howell Book House, 1988.

Carol Lea Benjamin. *Mother Knows Best, The Natural Way to Train Your Dog*. New York, NY, Howell Book House, 1985.

Jean Craighead George. *How to Talk to Your Dog*. New York, NY, Warner Books, 1985.

Jeanette Grainger and Connie Moore. *Natural Insect Repellents for Pets, People and Plants*. Austin, TX, The Herb Bar, 1991.

Joan Harper. *The Healthy Cat and Dog Cookbook*. Richland Center, WI, Pet Press, 1988.

Juliette de Bairacli Levy. *The Complete Herbal Handbook for the Dog and Cat*, Sixth Edition. London and Boston, Faber and Faber, Ltd., 1991.

Monks of New Skete. *The Art of Raising a Puppy*. Boston, New York, Toronto and London, Little Brown and Co., 1991.

Monks of New Skete. *How to Be Your Dog's Best Friend: A Training Manual for Dog Owners*. Boston, New York, Toronto, and London, Little Brown and Co., 1978.

Richard H. Pitcairn, DVM, Ph.D. "A New Look at the Vaccine Question." Eugene, OR, *Animal Natural Health*, undated article.

Richard H. Pitcairn, DVM, Ph.D. "Homeopathic Alternative to Vaccines." Eugene, OR, *Animal Natural Health*, undated article.

Richard Pitcairn, DVM, and Susan Hubble Pitcairn. *Dr. Pitcairn's Complete Guide to Natural Health for Dogs and Cats*. Emmaus, PA, Rodale Press, 1995.

Alfred Plechner, DVM. *Pet Allergies: Remedies for an Epidemic*. Inglewood, CA, Very Healthy Enterprises, 1986.

Diane Stein. *The Natural Remedy Book for Dogs and Cats*. Freedom, CA, The Crossing Press, 1994.

Diane Stein. *Natural Healing for Dogs and Cats*. Freedom, CA, The Crossing Press, 1993.

resources

Referrals

Academy of Veterinary Homeopathy
Larry Bernstein, VMD
751 NE 168 St.
N. Miami Beach, FL 33162-2427
(305) 652-5372
E-mail: natural@naturalholistic.com
web site: www.acadvethom.org

International Veterinary Acupuncture
   Society (IVAS)
268 W 3rd St. Suite #4
POB 2074
Nederland, CO 80466
(303) 258-3767

American Holistic Veterinary Medical
   Association (AHVMA)
2214 Old Emmorton Rd.
Bel Air, D 21015
(410) 569-0795
Fax: (410) 569-2346
E-mail: ahvma@compuserve.com
web site: www.AltVetMed.com

American Veterinary Chiropractic Assoc.
   (AVCA)
POB 249
Port Byron, IL 61275
(309) 523-3995

National Center for Homeopathy
801 N. Fairfax St. Suite 306
Alexandria, VA 22314
(703) 548-7790

Alternatives for Animals, L.C.
Referral Service
POB 1641
Brighton, MI 48116
(800) 424-8044

Greyhound Pets of America
Greyhound adoption
5 Carleton Ave.
Randolph, MA 02368
(800) 366-1472

Project BREED
Purebreed Rescue Referral
18707 Curry Powder Lane
Germantown, MD 20874-2014
(301) 428-3675

American Kennel Club (AKC)
51 Madison Ave.
New York, NY 10010
(212) 696-8200

Pet Sitters International
Locator Line—Referrals
418 E. King St.
King, NC 27021
(800) 268-7487

Other Information

Natural Pest Control Council of America
25 56th St. S.
St. Petersburg, FL 33707
(800) 858-7378

Fleabusters Rx for Fleas
10801 National Blvd, Suite 200
Los Angeles, CA 90064
(800) 846-3532
(310) 470-3532

Harmony Farm Supply
Natural Pest Control Products
POB 460
Graton, CA 95444
(707) 823-9125

The Herb Bar
Natural Pest Control Products
200 West Mary
Austin, TX 78704
(800) 766-4372

Homeopathic Educational Services
2124 Kittridge St.
Berkeley, CA 94704
(510) 649-0294
(800) 359-9051

Newton Homeopathic Laboratories
2360 Rockaway Ind. Blvd.
Conyers, GA 30207
(800) 448-7256

Hahnemann Pharmacy
828 San Pablo Ave.
Albany, CA 94706
(510) 527-3003

HVS Laboratories, Inc.
HomeoVetix
4584 Enterprise Ave.
Naples, FL 33941
(800) 521-7722

Pet Homeopathy Home Study
British Institute of Homeopathy
520 Washington Blvd. St. 423
Marina Del Rey, CA 90292
(800) 498-6323

National Animal Poison Control Center
College of Veterinary Medicine
University of Illinois at Urbana-
   Champagne
(900) 680-0000 $2.95/minute
(800) 548-2423 credit card

University of California, Davis
The Human-Animal Program
Grief Support
(916) 752-7418 (M-F 6:30-9:30 PM)

Cornell University
College of Veterinary Medicine
Pet Loss Support Hotline
(607) 253-3932 (Tues-Th 6-9PM)

The Furry Traveler
Puplication and Travel Club
(301) 495-4823

Vacationing with Your Pet
Directory $19.95
POB 8459
Scottsdale, AZ 85252
(800) 638-3637

Pets-R-Permitted Directory
ACI $11.95
POB 3930
Torrance, CA 90510

Pet Travel Resources
2327 Ward Rd.
Pocomoke, MD 21851
(410) 632-3944

Lorelei Resort
10273 Gulf Blvd.
Treasure Island, FL 33706
(813) 360-4351
(800) 354-6364

Products

Arthroflex
Pet Arthritis support
Long Life Catalog Co.
(888) NATURE-1

Hip and Joint Support—The Pet Project
505 S. Beverly Dr. #428
Beverly Hills, CA 90212
(310) 277-6120

Essential Reiki Journal
Essential Flower Essences by Diane Stein
POB 1436
Olney, MD 20830-1436
(301) 570-1990

index

BOOKS BY THE CROSSING PRESS

Natural Healing for Dogs and Cats
By Diane Stein

This invaluable resource tells how to use nutrition, minerals, massage, herbs, homeopathy, acupuncture, acupressure, flower essences, and psychic healing for optimal health.

$16.95 • Paper • ISBN 0-89594-614-9

The Natural Remedy Book for Dogs & Cats
By Diane Stein

"An informative guide...sure to be effective in reducing veterinary costs, while enhancing your relationship with your furry loved one."—NAPRA Trade Journal

$16.95 • Paper • ISBN 0-89594-686-6

Psycho Kitty?
Understanding Your Cat's "Crazy" Behavior
By Pam Johnson-Bennett

Johnson-Bennett shares real cases to illustrate various problems and explains how she arrives at an appropriate solution through behavior modification.

$12.95 • Paper • ISBN 0-89594-909-1

Bark Busters
Solving Your Dog's Behavioral Problems
By Sylvia Wilson

This step-by-step guide will help you improve your relationship with your pet. The simple, effective techniques are designed to work together with a dog's natural instincts, without cruelty.

$12.95 • Paper • ISBN 0-89594-881-8

To receive a current catalog from The Crossing Press
please call toll-free, 800-777-1048.
Visit our Web site on the Internet: www. crossingpress.com